W9-AKC-270

STITCHED

RAW EDGE

APPLIQUÉ

Sue Nickels & Pat Holly

Located in Paducah, Kentucky, the American Quilter's Society (AQS) is dedicated to promoting the accomplishments of today's quilters. Through its publications and events, AQS strives to honor today's quiltmakers and their work and to inspire future creativity and innovation in quiltmaking.

Editor: Barbara Smith
Copy Editor: Chrystal Abhalter
Graphic Design: Amy Chase
Cover Design: Michael Buckingham
Quilt Photos: Charles R. Lynch

Library of Congress Cataloging-in-Publication Data

Nickels, Sue.
    Stitched raw edge appliqué / by Sue Nickels and Pat Holly.
        p. cm.
    ISBN 1-57432-899-9
    1. Machine appliqué. I. Holly, Pat. II. Title.

TT779.N54 2006
746.44'5--dc22

2005034597

Additional copies of this book may be ordered from the American Quilter's Society, PO Box 3290, Paducah, KY 42002-3290, or call 1-800-626-5420 or online at www.AmericanQuilter.com.

Copyright ©2006, Sue Nickels

All rights reserved. No part of this book may be reproduced, stored in any retrieval system, or transmitted in any form, or by any means including but not limited to electronic, mechanical, photocopy, recording, or otherwise, without the written consent of the author and publisher. Patterns may be copied for personal use only.

Proudly printed and bound in the
United States of America

Dedication

This book is dedicated to our dad, Gerald Holly (1924–2003)
for encouraging us to be anything we wanted to be,
for being a great role model by always doing his very best,
and for loving our quilts and our successes with them!

Pilot dad, October 1944

Background: THE SPACE QUILT (87" x 87"), by Sue Nickels and Pat Holly, 2003. The full quilt is shown on page 8. This quilt was made as a tribute to our dad. He was a lieutenant in the Thirteenth Air Force, flew P-38s during World War II, and was a test pilot after the war. He chose to pursue a career as an engineer. His love of flying and his interest in NASA encouraged us to watch all the launches. This gave us a great appreciation of the importance of space exploration. We made this quilt to honor him as well as document the U.S. Space Program, the astronauts, and everyone associated with NASA.

Acknowledgments

We would like to thank the following people who have helped us throughout the process of writing this book. We could not have done it without their support.

To our editor, Barbara Smith, thank you for your patience and expert guidance.

To the American Quilter's Society, thank you for your continued support of quilters and for encouraging quiltmaking through many venues, including producing quilt shows, publishing books, and expanding into the television market.

To Bernina® of America, thank you for the use of your wonderful machines. Machine techniques are made easier by using the best tools available.

To our families: our husbands, Tim Nickels and Jack Mozdzen, and our daughters, Jessi, Ashley, Emmy, and Alyssa. Thank you for the little things you all have done to help us along the way.

To our supportive friends who are always ready to help with various tasks.

Pat would like to thank Mary Koval for her wonderful fabric contribution used in FOLKY FEATHERS AND FLOWERPOTS.

CONTENTS

INTRODUCTION

Welcome to the wonderful world of raw-edge fusible machine appliqué. Pat and I love this technique and know you will too. We have used this particular method for more than ten years and believe it has opened the doors for creativity and design options. We began our journey into appliqué about twenty-five years ago. For my daughter, Pat made a wonderful small baby quilt that was machine appliquéd (photo 1). She used a straight-stitch method with turned edges for the appliqué blocks. This was the first quilt Pat had made, and it inspired both of us to pursue quilting. We did this with a passion, exploring hand techniques for piecing, quilting, and appliqué. We enjoyed learning needle-turn hand appliqué under the expert guidance of our teacher and mentor, Gwen Marston, a fellow Michigan quilter. We absolutely fell in love with appliqué!

Photo 1. JESSI'S BABY QUILT (50" x 50"), 1978, by Pat Holly. This quilt was machine pieced, appliquéd, and quilted.

Because Pat and I have been sewers our whole lives, it was inevitable that we would turn to the sewing machine for quilting. We both started machine piecing in the early 1980s. Next, Pat and I both became converts to machine quilting and fell in love with free-motion quilting. It was only a matter of time before we decided to explore machine techniques for appliqué. Having started with

needle-turn hand appliqué, I used an invisible method, with turned edges and invisible thread, for my machine appliqué. The result looked very much like hand appliqué. I continue to teach this method and still love the results (photo 2). My next machine appliqué method still had that comfortable turned edge and a blanket stitch, in a folky style. This technique gives the look seen on the Sunbonnet Sue quilts of the '30s. I still love this technique and find it appropriate for certain projects.

Photo 2. YELLOW ROSES (30" x 30"), 1991, by Sue Nickels. Machine appliquéd with an invisible method that creates a hand-appliquéd look.

In 1995, Pat and I started working on quilt projects together. As sisters, we found our design styles similar, our work ethic the same, and our technical abilities equal. We realized how much we loved machine appliqué, but our designs were becoming more intricate and complicated. It was becoming increasingly tiresome to use a turned-edge technique with some of the smaller detailed pieces. We thought how nice it would be if we could become comfortable with a raw-edge method of machine appliqué. What made us uncomfortable with using a raw-edge technique? We did not like the idea of using a large amount of fusible in our quilts. Even if a quilt never makes it to a bed, we always believe we are making a bed quilt. We like the softness of quilts and think that quilts containing a lot of fusible become stiff and less quilt-like. We also did not like the heavy satin stitch commonly used along raw edges because it also added stiffness.

We needed to resolve these issues. Pat was the first to experiment. Her small quilt TOUCAN FRIENDS (photo 3) was her first attempt to use this raw-edge fusible technique, and she loved it. To reduce the amount of fusible in the project, she used only an edging of it. A small blanket stitch was then used to secure the raw edges. This method creates a secure edge, but it is still soft and quilt-like. I wasn't so easily convinced. In our quilt BLACKBIRDS FLY (photo 4), made in 1996, Pat used this raw-edge fusible method on her blocks, but I used my turned-edge folky method for my floral blocks. After seeing how well done her blocks were, I became a convert and started using this method often.

Photo 4. BLACKBIRDS FLY (90" x 90"), 1996, machine pieced, appliquéd, and quilted by Sue Nickels and Pat Holly. The blackbird blocks were done with raw-edge fusible appliqué. The floral blocks have turned edges.

Photo 3. TOUCAN FRIENDS (21½" x 26"), 1993, machine pieced, machine appliquéd, and machine quilted by Pat Holly.

The wonder of this method was revealed to me with our next collaboration. The original designs were very small and intricate, and I believe we would not have made our elaborate BEATLES QUILT if it were not for this method. We

were so surprised when this quilt won the prestigious American Quilter's Society Best of Show award in 1998. Pat's quilt THE FAB FOUR (photo 5) features birds in the same style as those that appear on the BEATLES QUILT.

Photo 5. THE FAB FOUR (detail). The full quilt is shown on page 55.

Pat and I continue to collaborate and mainly use this method for machine appliqué. Our quilt NEW YORK STATE OF MIND (photo 6, page 8) was made for an invitational exhibit, which provided a wonderful opportunity for us to combine our machine techniques in a unique project. This quilt was machine pieced by Pat, machine appliquéd by both of us, and I did the machine quilting. We also collaborated on a quilt called THE JUBILEE ALBUM QUILT (photo 7, page 8), which was featured in a major magazine and helped promote the popularity of machine appliqué.

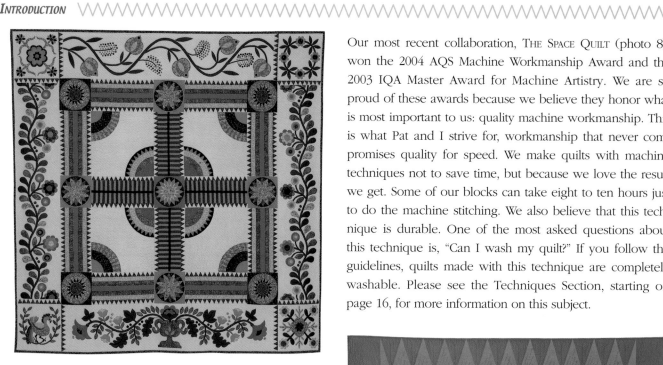

Photo 6. NEW YORK STATE OF MIND (69" x 69"), 2000, machine made by Sue Nickels and Pat Holly. The raw-edge method was used for this quilt.

Photo 7. THE JUBILEE ALBUM QUILT (79" x 91"), 2002, by Pat Holly and Sue Nickels. This quilt was made entirely by machine. The raw-edge fusible method was used for the appliqué. There are surface embellishments on some of the appliqué pieces.

Our most recent collaboration, THE SPACE QUILT (photo 8), won the 2004 AQS Machine Workmanship Award and the 2003 IQA Master Award for Machine Artistry. We are so proud of these awards because we believe they honor what is most important to us: quality machine workmanship. This is what Pat and I strive for, workmanship that never compromises quality for speed. We make quilts with machine techniques not to save time, but because we love the result we get. Some of our blocks can take eight to ten hours just to do the machine stitching. We also believe that this technique is durable. One of the most asked questions about this technique is, "Can I wash my quilt?" If you follow the guidelines, quilts made with this technique are completely washable. Please see the Techniques Section, starting on page 16, for more information on this subject.

Photo 8. THE SPACE QUILT (91" x 91"), 2003, by Sue Nickels and Pat Holly. The future block has more than 360 circles, stitched successfully with the raw-edge fusible method and patience!

Pat and I are excited to share this technique. We have used it successfully for more than ten years. We believe that we could not make the type of quilts we want without this method, and it has opened the doors to design possibilities. We love and admire all types of appliqué quilts and feel fortunate that there are many choices available to quilters today. For the quilters who already love machine techniques or for those who are ready to try machine techniques for the first time, this book is for you. We hope you enjoy the technique, your machine, and our patterns!

Sue Nickels

INSPIRATION

We have reached the point where we love designing all aspects of our quilts. How do we get our ideas? It helps to keep an open mind and be observant of everything around you. Not only do we look carefully at any antique quilt we come across, we are also excited to see old embroideries, textiles, and even wood carvings on old furniture. We have been lucky enough to be able to travel, and make it a point to go to museums or old houses. Who knows what piece of pottery or bit of cloth will motivate our creativity and invigorate our imaginations?

I take a lot of pictures, first making sure this is permitted. In the event that photography is not allowed, we always bring paper and pencil along. I have been known to make quick sketches of a portion of an altar cloth, tile floor, or intricate carving on a wooden church pew. We are always looking to expand our collection of antique quilts, concentrating on those with visible machine stitches and appliqué as well as quilting. Expand your viewing realm! Look at textiles from all over the world. I look for historical books from other countries and marvel at the uniqueness of the designs. Once you begin to open your eyes to what is around you, you will find unlimited riches to spark your creative endeavors.

I keep a sketchbook handy at all times. Sometimes I'll sit down with one of my books of world textiles and look carefully at the photos for specific details. I love to look for bird images, for example. I'll sketch these in my book and have them as a starting point for a drawing. I don't usually copy a figure exactly but use the image as a beginning. Most of my reference books are of antique items. Please don't copy any recent (within the last 75 years) quilts or other artwork without proper permission. Look at every part of these old textiles: the edge treatments, color choices, layouts, and so on. There are so many opportunities for inspiration, you are sure to find something that catches your eye.

My book collection includes any quilt books I can find with pictures of antique quilts. The state documentation project books are full of wonderful old quilts. I also collect books about textiles from countries around the world. A great place to find this type of book is in museum bookstores. I have found art books from museum collections that show old textiles from pieces that may not be on display.

An annual favorite that is no longer being published was the *Quilt Engagement Calendar*. Most of the quilts were antiques. One of my friends found a collection of these calendars for sale online, so you can still find copies if you are persistent. When attending quilt shows, I always visit the antique quilt dealers. Not only do I look for old quilts to collect, I look for ideas. I always ask permission before taking any photographs. Antique quilts are great to study. The obvious freedom these quiltmakers felt when designing their quilts is something we should all try to emulate. A basic component like leaves or stems can be interpreted in so many ways. Sometimes you can find many ideas looking at a single quilt.

Let's look at some of the antique quilts we have collected. Two of the quilts are in the four-block format, both with a wreath design. The FOUR BLOCK ROSE WREATH has soft shades of pink, tan, and green (photo 9). Four giant buds come off the circle, flanked by two roses. I love the two sizes of leaves, giant and tiny. Notice that the placement of the roses and leaves that come off the bud is slightly different in each corner of the block. This relaxed approach to placement gives the quilt its charm and liveliness.

Photo 9. FOUR BLOCK ROSE WREATH (70" x 70"), owned by Pat Holly. This hand-appliquéd, machine-quilted piece has turned edges with straight-stitch machine appliqué.

The FOUR-BLOCK TULIP WREATH has some of that same freedom (photo 10). This quilt also provides an example of being creative in designing floral elements. Look at just one of the wreaths. There are two tulip stems with leaves going into the center of the circle and two other shapes. I think each shape is a bud-leaves-stem unit all rolled into one, and what fun they are to look at. Compare the two wreath quilts. Look at how they are similar: wreaths; four flowers placed at the top, bottom, and sides of the circle; stems going out to the four corners of the block. Then notice how they are different: one has only a single large flower in the center of the circle. In addition, the placement, size, and style of leaves differ. The type of flower is also different. One quilt has a large, plain border. One has no border at all. Think about what type of four-block wreath design you could create.

Photo 10. FOUR-BLOCK TULIP WREATH (65" x 72"), owned by Sue Nickels. This piece has turned-edges with straight-stitch machine appliqué. It is machine pieced and hand quilted.

The RED AND TAN CROSSED FLOWERS antique quilt is an example of blocks set on point (photo 11). This setting alone changes the whole look of a quilt compared to one with a straight set. The big red-and-white blocks seem to form a white cross or, if you step back farther, the triangles form a star. The appliqué blocks are uniquely arranged. Why only three flowers? Why not have flowers in each corner? The direction the appliqué

blocks are pointing is worth noting. Three of the blocks face one direction, the rest point the other way. Then, the corner triangles were left vacant, without any red triangles or curvy pieces. I think it is fun to ponder why these quilters made the decisions they did.

Photo 11. RED AND TAN CROSSED FLOWERS (80" x 80"), owned by Pat Holly. The appliqué has a turned edge, and it was straight-stitched by machine, then hand quilted.

The first antique appliqué quilt I purchased was the TREE OF LIFE (photo 12, page 11). Unlike the rest of the antique quilts we are showing you, this one was completely made by hand. The others have visible machine stitches. I remember being stunned by this quilt. The six-block arrangement is not that common. I had never seen this type of flowering tree design before. The split in the middle of the branches is unusual, and the little branches sprouting from the bottom add a fun rhythm to that area of the quilt. It reminds me of having to chop off the sprouts from the base of my flowering crabapple tree every year. The outer border is also worth noting. One side has a tiny vine border. Two sides have a larger vine, and the last side has no border at all. I like that idea and have used it in some of my quilts.

The TULIP WITH TULIP AND HEART BORDER shows a great block arrangement (photo 13, page 11). It is even a little difficult to see how the blocks are placed. With the blocks set on point, the stems face many directions. It's

Photo 12. TREE OF LIFE (82" x 101"), owned by Pat Holly. It is hand appliquéd and hand quilted.

fun to see that even the side and corner setting triangles have varying sizes and arrangements of the tulips, stems, and leaves. The wonderful borders have different sizes of tulips, and the tiny side borders, with the hearts and leaves, add a perfect frame to this quilt.

The combined pieced and appliquéd NEW YORK BEAUTY antique quilt is a great example of a traditional design that has been allowed a bit of freedom (photo 14). The flower spray in the center of each block is one addition. The large red spiky fans in the corners are definitely a loosened up variation of the usual treatment. Something to note is the use of straight-stitch machine appliqué to create the pointy triangle sashing units. These are usually hand or machine pieced with precision, but when you look closely at this quilt, you see that these triangles, as well as the points along the edge of the red fans and the flower spray, are all machine appliquéd. So, not only do you find freedom in the design decisions, but also you see that the quiltmaker made a bold choice in sewing technique as well.

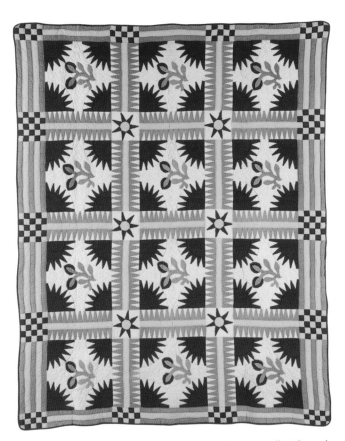

Photo 13. TULIP WITH TULIP AND HEART BORDER (65" x 72"), owned by Sue Nickels. The maker used straight-stitch machine stitching on the turned-edge appliqué. Then she hand quilted the layers.

Photo 14. NEW YORK BEAUTY (74" x 90"), owned by Pat Holly. The techniques used include turned edges, straight-stitch machine appliqué, machine piecing, and hand quilting.

Examples of how we have used the inspiration from antique quilts can be seen in our JUBILEE ALBUM QUILT (page 8) and ANNIVERSARY QUILT (photo 15). The blocks in THE JUBILEE ALBUM QUILT were designed by using antique quilt blocks from many different quilts as inspiration. The color scheme for that quilt came from a completely different antique quilt. I thought that the red, white, blue, and yellow together created a fresh combination and brought in the patriotic connection.

Our NEW YORK STATE OF MIND quilt (page 8) contains a vibrant gold, orange, red, and green color selection. This idea came from looking at great Pennsylvania German designs. Some of the border appliqué ideas came from one of our favorite quiltmakers from the past, Susan McCord. The ANNIVERSARY QUILT idea came from a quilt I saw in an old *Quilt Engagement Calendar*. I particularly loved the soft color palette and looked specifically for fabrics in those subtle tan, blue, and green colors. The loopy edge treatment came from an old quilt that had a lacey border. I was not interested in adding lace to the edge but liked the idea of something open and loose, hence the loops.

I hope this discussion gives you an idea of how Sue and I come up with ideas for our quilts. Remember to look for something you respond to, and enjoy the same freedom the quiltmakers of the past so beautifully demonstrate.

Pat Holly

Photo 15. ANNIVERSARY QUILT (57" x 57") 2005, by Sue Nickels and Pat Holly. This quilt, which was inspired by an antique quilt, is made entirely by machine. .

Raw-Edge Applique Basics

Supplies

A good understanding of supplies is essential for success in quilting projects. Refer to the Authors' Favorite Tools, page 94, for a list of products we prefer.

Preparation Supplies

Circle-maker template

Use this drafting tool for drawing small circles accurately.

Iron

A good iron is essential for machine appliqué. Have a good understanding of the heat settings on your iron.

Ironing board

A sturdy ironing board with a hard surface is recommended. Use a muslin cover because the ironing surface could become discolored from the heat, starch build-up, and the occasional fusible mishap.

Light box

Use this box for positioning appliqué pieces on dark or busy fabric.

Fusible web

Select a lightweight product with paper on one side and fusible web on the other. Heat is used to adhere the web to the fabric in a two-step process. Cut the fusible web into manageable-sized squares. Store them flat in plastic. Careful handling will help keep the web from separating from the paper. Do not fold or roll. Follow the manufacturer's guidelines for heat settings and length of time to fuse.

Pencils

Use a sharp lead pencil to draw the appliqué patterns on paper-backed fusible web, a fabric marking pencil to mark the fabric, and chalk pencils to mark guidelines for surface embellishments.

Pressing sheet

An appliqué pressing sheet will prove invaluable for preparing more complex units before placing them on a background. Fusible products will not stick to the surface of a pressing sheet.

Rulers

Use acrylic rotary-cutting rulers for measuring and to mark guidelines for surface embellishments.

Scissors

Small embroidery scissors are essential to achieve accuracy when cutting intricate appliqué pieces. Also use good-quality small scissors when cutting paper-backed fusible shapes. Using dull paper scissors may cause the fusible to separate from the paper. Designate a pair of embroidery scissors for cutting only fusibles. You may have to replace them occasionally, depending on how much you use this technique.

Spray starch

Spray starch is used to stabilize the background. A light application is helpful on the appliqué fabric as well. All brands are equal; however, a regular-weight starch is preferred. Sizing is a different product from starch. We use starch.

Straight pins

Use sharp straight pins to hold bias-strip stems in place before thread basting them to the background. Also, use straight pins to carefully adjust appliqué pieces on the background.

Stiletto

This sharp, pointed tool is used to position appliqué pieces on the background. It can also be used to assist in pulling threads to the back of the piece.

Template plastic

Use a heat-resistant plastic template as an aid in pressing scalloped edges.

Tracing paper

Trace your chosen pattern on tracing paper to create a full-sized pattern and use it as an overlay on the block to position appliqué pieces. Tracing paper is also ideal for asymmetrical designs because the drawing can be turned over for tracing or positioning from the reverse side.

Turning tool

This tool is used for turning bias tubes right side out.

Tweezers

Use tweezers for holding small appliqué pieces for cutting. Also use them for picking up and positioning pieces on the background. Select very sharp pointed tweezers. Regular pointed and reverse-action tweezers are also needed (fig. 1).

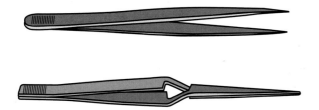

Fig. 1. Regular and reverse-action tweezers

Sewing Supplies

Curved-point scissors

These special scissors, or snippers, are great for clipping threads after sewing the appliqué pieces (fig. 2). They work quickly because they have a spring action, and you don't need to put your fingers in and out of scissor holes. They can also be used for taking out stitching.

Fig. 2. Curved-point scissors

Self-threading needle

This needle can be used for bringing thread ends to the back of the block (fig. 3). It is our favorite notion and stays by the machine at all times. There is a small opening at the top of the needle that allows the thread to pop into the needle eye, saving time that would be used in threading the needle.

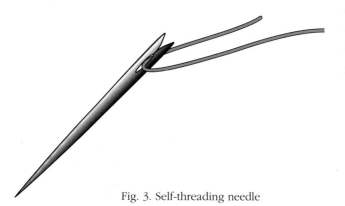

Fig. 3. Self-threading needle

Sewing machine

Use a good quality sewing machine for machine appliqué. Provide yearly maintenance and keep the machine cleaned and oiled. The blanket stitch is the main stitch used for this technique. A zigzag stitch can also be used. The straight stitch is used for some of the stems.

It is helpful to have a needle-down option and a variable needle position option. A presser-foot knee lift or pivot position option is also helpful for pivoting easily along the edge of the appliqué pieces. These features are not mandatory, but they are helpful for accurate machine appliqué.

It is also helpful to have a large work surface. A sewing machine that sits in a cabinet is nice because the block is completely supported during stitching. If your machine sits on a tabletop, a large acrylic extension table can be helpful because it will support the block for stitching.

Sewing machine feet

An open-toed appliqué foot is a must for machine appliqué. It looks like a regular presser foot but without the bar in front. A darning foot is used for free-motion stitching, and a zipper foot is used for piped and corded edges (fig. 4).

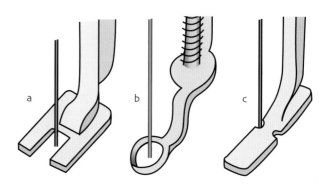

Fig. 4. Machine feet: (a) open-toed foot, (b) darning foot, (c) zipper foot

Sewing machine needles and thread

The needle size depends on the weight of the thread used. We use the following chart as a guide. (Weights of threads are not always consistent, so these guidelines may need to be altered accordingly.)

Thread Weight	Needle Size
60 weight	70/10
50 weight	70/10 or 80/12
40 weight	80/12
30 weight	90/14

The type of needle used depends on the type of fabric. Universal needles work pretty well for all types of fabric. Sharper needles are recommended for stitching on light-weight woven cotton fabric, which is what most quilters use. A needle called a "sharp" works well for machine appliquéing cotton fabrics. Change your needle often. A dull needle will cause poor-quality stitching.

Sewing machine needle case

This small case holds packages of machine needles and has a place to indicate what type of needle is in the machine.

Tapestry needle

Large-eyed needles (size 18 or 20) are used to pull heavy threads to the back of the block.

Appliqué threads

Use only good-quality thread. Use a thread in a matching color to blend with the appliqué piece. A contrasting thread color can be used for a decorative look. Use the same thread color in the bobbin that is used on top.

Cotton thread (40-weight): This slightly heavier than average-weight thread looks very nice and covers the raw edge.

Cotton thread (50-weight): This average-weight thread also covers the raw edge nicely and is a favorite.

Cotton thread (60-weight): This fine embroidery thread works well for surface work on the background block. It is very fine and will not make the background block heavier. Because it is thin, it will not cover the raw edge for the appliqué technique.

Decorative threads

There are many decorative threads available to quilters today. These threads are a nice choice for machine appliqué techniques. Test the threads first to see if you like the look before stitching your block. The choices include polyester, rayon, metallic, silk, and acrylic threads.

Fine machine embroidery threads offer a wide range of color choices and work well for surface work. Variegated threads can give a pleasing, subtle effect in machine appliqué. Some of these threads come on unusual spools and may need to be fed to the sewing machine with an auxiliary guide to achieve a smooth threading path. Spool stands and auxiliary guides are available.

Perle cotton thread

Use this thread to make thread stems. It comes in many colors and weights (fig. 5).

Fig. 5. Different weights of perle cotton

Cording

Cord is used for the filling in a piped edge. It comes in different sizes and fiber contents.

Lip cord

You can find this trim in the upholstery area of your fabric store. It is a fancy cord that has a seam allowance added to it. It can be used to create a unique quilt edge.

Fabric

We use 100 percent cotton. Fabrics with a different fiber content may produce varied results. Test your fabrics to make sure that the colors will not run or bleed onto other fabrics before using them in your quilt. Prewash cotton fabrics before using them. A lot of time will be spent making a beautiful quilt, so use the best fabric you can.

Fabric selection is very personal. Choosing the background fabric carefully is essential because this is the largest amount of fabric in the quilt. If you are doing surface work on the background, a solid or tone-on-tone would be a good choice.

Select a wide variety of fabrics for the appliqué pieces. Vary the scale, choosing small- to large-scale prints. Do a lot of auditioning of fabric throughout the process. Sometimes it is difficult to determine if a fabric will work until it has been cut out and placed with the other pieces.

In hand appliqué, many quilters have been told that the grain line of the appliqué fabric should match the grain line of the background block. It would be difficult to do this on quilts that have a lot of little pieces, such as the ones in this book. If the appliqué piece is large, a basket for example, it will look better if the basket grain line matches the background grain line (fig. 6).

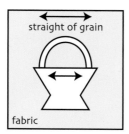

Fig. 6. Matching basket and background grain lines

For smaller pieces, choose the best look for that particular piece. For example, a stripe or directional print might look better one way versus the other. When using small prints and solids, choose the best placement of the appliqué template to minimize wasting fabric.

Appliqué Techniques

It's a good idea to read this whole section to have a full understanding of the techniques before proceeding to your quilt project.

The raw-edge fusible method is a wonderful choice for machine appliqué. It is perfect for intricate appliqué designs that have small, fussy pieces. The results are accurate and precise with sharp points and neat edges. There are no seam allowances to turn under, so preparation time is reduced. Although this technique works well for intricate designs, it is also appropriate for simple, classic appliqué.

In the past, some quilters have not liked the final result when using the raw-edge fusible machine appliqué method. When fusible web is used throughout the appliqué piece, the quilt becomes less pliable, particularly when used in multiple layers. With our technique, most of the fusible is cut away, leaving a ¼" outline of web on the outside edge of the appliqué piece. The result is a softer finished product.

Another reason some quilters have not liked the raw-edge method is that the satin stitch normally used along the edge of the appliqué made it stiffer. With our method, a small blanket stitch has been used to cover the raw edge of the appliqué piece, creating a lovely look and a softer finished edge. A small zigzag stitch can also be used if your machine does not have a blanket stitch.

We will show you the methods we use to achieve quality work. These methods are not difficult. We do not rush through our projects. They do take time and patience. We really do all of the steps we talk about, all of the time. We are often asked, "Isn't this really hard to do?" We don't think any of it is hard. Some of the designs have many pieces, but the basic method is easy.

For the beginner, choose a simple pattern to start or do a small practice piece with a few flowers and leaves to learn the technique.

Making a Master Pattern

Choose a pattern (patterns begin on page 50) and trace it on tracing paper. If you prefer to photocopy, you can enlarge or reduce the pattern for your project. Note that, for asymmetrical designs, the pattern will be the mirror image of the finished quilt.

Tracing. Cut a piece of tracing paper the same size as your background square.

Fold the tracing paper in half in one direction and then the other to find the center.

Align the center of the tracing paper with the center of the pattern.

Trace the pattern from the book with a sharp pencil.

Photocopy. Photocopying shops need to have permission, which is at the bottom of the copyright page in the front of the book. Make your photocopy on see-through paper or vellum. For very large projects, you may need to tape several copies together to make a master of the whole design.

Marking Fusible Web

We have used paper-backed fusible web for the quilts in this book. Please have enough available for each project.

Use a sharp pencil to trace the individual pattern pieces on the paper side of the fusible web. Space the pieces about ½" apart. To help you keep track, write a small number on each pattern piece and the same number on the corresponding fusible web piece. To make sure the number won't get cut off in the next step, write close to the pattern line.

Cutting Fusible Web

To reduce the amount of fusible used in the project, you will be cutting a pattern shape from the fusible for each appliqué piece then cutting the center out of the fusible shape. The resulting piece will be referred to as a "fusible open shape."

With small embroidery scissors, cut about ¼" (by eye) outside the traced pattern line. Next, cut directly through the drawn line to access the area inside the line. Cut out the inner area a scant ¼" from the traced pattern line to complete the open shape (fig. 7). Repeat the process to prepare the fusible open shapes for all the appliqué pieces in the block. Small pieces, such as tiny circles and narrow stems, do not need to have their centers cut out.

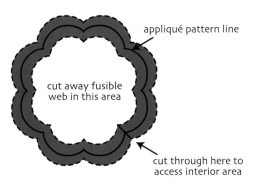

Fig. 7. Fusible open shape. Cut the web on both sides of the drawn pattern line, as shown by dashed lines.

Fusing Open Shapes

Choose your appliqué fabric. Lightly starch the fabric from the back. One light application is all that is needed to help stabilize the appliqué pieces.

Place the prepared open shape on the back of the fabric. Keep the paper side up and the fusible side down. (If you prefer to place appliqués according to fabric grain line, refer to pages 15–16.)

Following the manufacturer's directions, fuse the open shape to the fabric (fig. 8). Be careful! If the fusible side is facing up, it will fuse to the iron. This first fusing does not melt the glue completely. It only transfers it to the back of the fabric.

Some quilters use an appliqué pressing sheet during this step. This sheet ensures that the web glue does not adhere to the iron or ironing board. We do not use a

pressing sheet, however. Instead, we have an iron and ironing surface used only for machine appliqué.

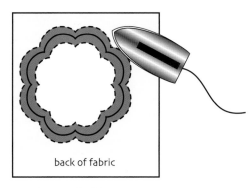

Fig. 8. Fusing an open shape to the fabric

Pat's Pointers

Storing fusible open shapes. A good way to keep track of the open shapes is to store them in small self-closing plastic bags or little envelopes. The bags or envelopes will protect the web pieces from separating from the paper backing. Be sure to keep everything nice and flat.

Sue's Solutions

Positioning large open shapes. When placing the fusible open shapes for large appliqué pieces on fabric, follow these steps: Place the open shape, fusible side down on the back of the fabric. Because large open shapes are easily distorted, lay the tracing-paper master pattern on top of the shape to make sure the placement is accurate. Once the shape placement is correct, tap lightly with a dry, hot iron directly on top of the master pattern to tack the open shape in place. Remove the master pattern and fuse the open shape to the appliqué fabric. For an example of large pattern pieces that will need to be handled this way, see the vase patterns in MORNING HAS BROKEN on page 73.

Cutting Appliqué Pieces

With the same small embroidery scissors, cut through the fusible and the appliqué fabric on the traced pattern line (fig. 9, page 18). The extra fusible web that is beyond the pattern line ensures that there will be fusible web all the way out to the cut raw edge. This method seals the edge with the fusible and reduces the chance of fraying.

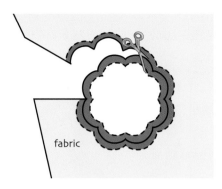

Fig. 9. Cut the appliqué on the traced line.

Sue's Solutions

Overlapping appliqué pieces. These need special consideration, and Pat and I approach this subject somewhat differently. Here is the method I use:

Notice which appliqué pieces lie underneath other pieces. The patterns have double hash marks (shown in red in the figure) to indicate that an edge lies under another piece.

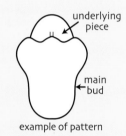

Trace the individual patterns on the paper side of the fusible web, leaving at least ½" between pieces. Be sure to include the hash marks on the underlying pieces.

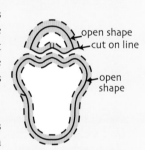

Cut the fusible open shapes as previously described on page 17, with the following exception: along an edge with hash marks, cut the fusible web directly on the traced line.

Fuse the open shape to the back of your chosen appliqué fabric. Cut the fabric piece on the traced lines, except for the edge with the hash marks. On that edge, add a ¼" allowance by eye as you cut.

Because the allowance has no fusible, there will not be a double fusible layer when the other piece is appliquéd over it.

Preparing Background Squares

During machine stitching, the edges of a block can fray and become distorted, so you need to cut the back-ground square about 2" bigger than the finished size of the block. For a 20" finished block, for example, you would cut the background square 22". After all the stitching is done, trim the block to the correct size, including seam allowances, to create a fresh, clean edge for sewing the blocks together.

For fusible appliqué, the background square requires a stabilizer. Spray a light coating of starch on the back of the square to stiffen it. Let the starch soak into the fabric. Carefully iron the square to dry the starch. A second application is usually needed. The background square should be the weight of light paper. A third application may be needed if the fabric is lightweight.

Pat's Pointers

Overlapping appliqué pieces. My method of handling overlapping pieces is similar to Sue's:

When tracing the pattern pieces on the fusible web, mark a dashed line on the underlying piece where the other piece overlaps it.

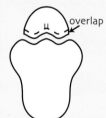

Extend the outside cutting line so it is about ⅛" to 3⁄16" beyond the dashed line. Be sure this area completely lies beyond the cutting edge so you will have enough fabric under the top piece.

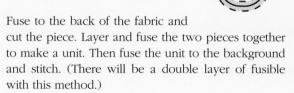

Cut the fusible out beyond the drawn line in the manner explained in Cutting Fusible Web (page 17).

Remove any web from the interior, if the piece is large enough.

Fuse to the back of the fabric and cut the piece. Layer and fuse the two pieces together to make a unit. Then fuse the unit to the background and stitch. (There will be a double layer of fusible with this method.)

Placing Appliqué Pieces

Center the background square over the master pattern. If the fabric is dark or busy, you can use a light box under the master pattern. As an alternative, you can use the master pattern as an overlay for positioning the appliqués. This method works nicely for blocks that are bigger than the light box.

Use a fabric pencil to mark guidelines for stems on the background. Baste the bias stems to the background first then stitch any thread stems. (See the various stems on pages 28–31.)

Make any multiple-layered units. Remove the paper backing from the appliqués. Place all of them accurately on the background square. Use a large straight pin or stiletto to help move the appliqués into place.

Make sure that overlapping pieces are properly placed. Then fuse them to the background by placing the iron over the appliqué pieces. (Be careful not to disturb their placement. Sliding the iron over the surface may move the appliqués.) Follow the ironing directions for your specific fusible web. Once pressed, the pieces cannot be moved. Turn the block over and iron it lightly from the back to be sure that the fusible web is heated evenly.

If you are working on a large block and positioning appliqué pieces away from your ironing board, you can avoid disturbing the placement of the appliqué pieces by bringing your iron to the work area and pressing very lightly to tack the pieces down. The block can then be carefully moved to the ironing board and pressed.

Blanket Stitch

The inspiration for this machine stitch comes from the blanket stitch used in hand appliqué. The machine version can be made quite small so that it covers the raw edge. We prefer the blanket stitch for our appliqué, sometimes called an appliqué stitch. It gives a beautiful edge finish to the appliqué pieces. Because there is no turn-under allowance, the appliqués look flatter. Colorful threads can be used to enhance this lovely stitch.

On most sewing machines the blanket stitch is made with the straight stitch on the right and the bite stitch to the left (fig. 10). Some sewing machines make the blanket stitch the opposite way, that is, the straight stitch is on the left and the bite stitch is to the right (fig. 11). If your machine has a mirror-image function, use it and the stitch will be made the more common way. If you don't have this option, the stitching can be done from the opposite direction for the same effect.

If your machine does not have a blanket stitch, a zigzag is another option. We use a flat zigzag to avoid the look

of the heavy satin stitch. The zigzag stitch looks different from the blanket stitch, but it works equally well.

Fig. 10. Stitching in mirror image

Fig. 11. Stitching with bite stitched to the right

Setting the Machine

The settings will vary from machine to machine. A good place to start is with a 2.0 width and a 2.0 length, which would measure about 1⁄16" by 1⁄16". A good rule of thumb is to set the length and width to the same number, although we often vary this slightly.

Pat's Pointers

Multiple-layered units. When preparing appliqué pieces that have multiple layers, some stitching can be done before fusing the pieces as a unit to the background square. As an example, a multiple-layered flower might include a large flower piece, smaller inner flower, and a center circle. Fuse the circle to the inner flower and the inner flower to the large flower, leaving the paper backing on the large flower. Stitch the edges of the center circle and inner flower to complete the unit, which is then ready to appliqué to the background.

When creating these layered units, sometimes you may need to remove the paper from all the pieces as you construct them. With all the paper removed, if you want to fuse some of the layers together, you will need to use a non-stick appliqué pressing sheet. If you don't, you will end up fusing the pieces to your ironing board … a fusible mishap!

Using a non-stick pressing sheet is a great aid when creating multiple-layered units. You can place the pattern under the see-through sheet, place the appliqué pieces right on top of the sheet, and fuse the pieces exactly where they belong. After letting the fabric cool down, gently peel the fused unit from the sheet and fuse it to the background.

Use an open-toed appliqué foot to have a clear view of the stitching. Thread the machine with the desired thread. We often use a thread color that matches the appliqué piece. Use the same thread color in the bobbin, so the bobbin thread will not show on the top if it pops up to the surface in some places. Be sure to practice on a sample piece of fabric first to achieve the desired settings and to become comfortable with the stitch.

The stitch length should be set so that the distance between the bites is close enough together that no fraying occurs, but not so close that it looks like a satin stitch, heavy with thread. The bite should cover about four to five threads of fabric on the raw edge (fig. 11, page 19). If the bite is too short and only covers one to two threads, the edge may be prone to fraying. (The bite is actually two stitches in the cycle, one stitch into the fabric and one back to the starting point of the bite.)

Making Neat Stitches

It is important to keep the straight stitch on the background very close to the appliqué piece. If the straight stitch is not right next to the appliqué, it can look sloppy. However, if the straight stitch is too close to the raw edge, this might also cause fraying (fig. 12).

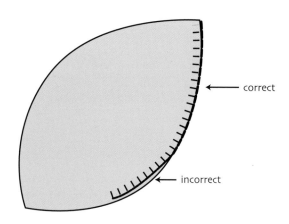

Fig. 12. Keep the straight stitch close to the appliqué piece.

Sue's Solutions

Variable needle position. I like to use the variable needle position feature to move the needle to the farthest right setting and then use the inside edge of the right toe on the open-toed appliqué foot to guide my stitching close to the edge of the piece. Pat prefers to have the needle in the center needle position and visually guide the stitch along the edge.

Checking Tension

Once the best stitch width and length have been determined, check the thread tension. If the bobbin thread shows on the top, loosen the top tension slightly. In other words, if the setting is at 4, move it to 3. Adjusting the top tension is usually sufficient to solve most tension problems. Rarely, the tension in the bobbin case may need adjusting. Refer to your sewing machine manual for instructions on doing this or consult your dealer.

Navigating Curves

An important part of successful blanket stitching is keeping the bite portion of the stitch perpendicular to the straight stitch (fig. 13).

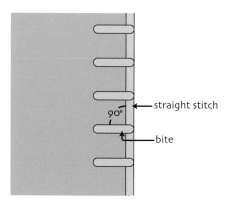

Fig. 13. Anatomy of a good blanket stitch

This is easy to do along a straight line, but most appliqué patterns have curved designs. When you are stitching along a curve, you will need to pivot to stay close to the edge of the appliqué and to keep the bite perpendicular to the straight stitch (fig. 14).

It is important to pivot when the needle is in the background. If you pivot with the needle in the appliqué, the bite will open and look like a "V" (fig. 15). If your machine has a needle-down option, always use it for the blanket stitch. This way the block will not move during pivoting.

Fig. 14. Correct pivoting in the background

Fig. 15. Incorrect pivoting in the appliqué

It is also important to learn the stitch cycle and be aware of where you are in it at all times. Start each piece at the same place in the blanket stitch. (We like to start in the background.) Some machines have a pattern-begin feature, and this can be used. Pivot often on curves. Small circles and tight curves may need pivoting every stitch pattern.

Stitching Outside Points

Perfecting the blanket stitch on outside and inside points takes practice, and a leaf has a good outside point for practicing (fig. 16). Always start far enough from the point so you have time to establish the stitch cycle before you get to the point. You must slow down and sew one stitch at a time as you approach the point. As you get up to the point, evaluate where the stitches are going to be by looking at what has already been stitched. Often, the last stitch in the background will exactly line up with the point.

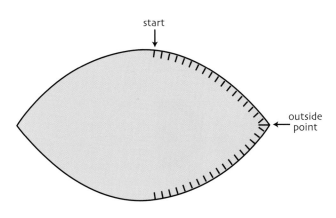

Fig. 16. Stitching an outside point

If the stitch is not going to hit exactly at the point, here is what you can do. Get as close to the point as you can, stopping at the place where the next stitch would go beyond the point. Bring the needle up and, as it comes down, hold back the fabric so it does not move as much as it wants to (as a normal stitch). Yes, it is okay to do this! The needle will go down close to the point. Stop at this position with the needle in the background. Pivot and take the bite portion of the stitch into the leaf, pivot again, then continue down the other side of the leaf. As you gain experience with this method, we promise it will get easier.

Stitching Inside Points

Flowers have good inside points for practice (fig. 17). Stitch along the edge of the flower until you come to an inside

point. Stop with the needle in the background. Remember to be aware of your position in the stitch cycle. You want to complete the straight stitch then pivot at the inside point. You can hold back the fabric, if necessary, to end the stitch cycle at the point. Pivot, take the bite stitch perpendicular to the point, pivot, and continue sewing.

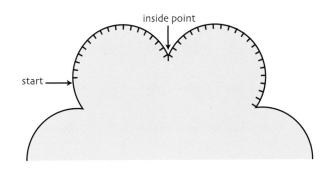

Fig. 17. Stitching an inside point

Starting and Stopping

Begin stitching the appliqué away from the point. As you begin, hold the top and bobbin threads behind the appliqué foot to keep them out of the way so they won't get tangled or sewn into the work when you start stitching. Sew around the appliqué and end the stitching at the exact spot where you started. A minor adjustment may be needed in the length of the last straight stitch.

Clip the threads, leaving at least a 6" tail. Pull the top two threads to the back of the block. Tie all four threads (top and bobbin) in a double knot (fig. 18). If the threads do not contrast with the background, simply clip the threads short.

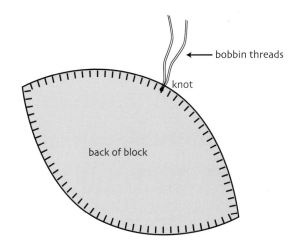

Fig. 18. Tie a knot.

To keep contrasting threads from showing through the background, thread the four tails into a self-threading needle and weave them into about three of the blanket stitches (fig. 19). Clip the threads close to the stitching. You will want to deal with thread ends immediately after completing each segment of stitching. If they are left to do later, you will find a mess of threads on the back.

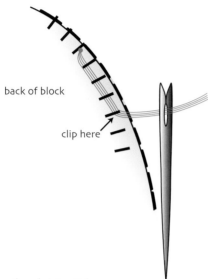

Fig. 19. Weave threads into stitches.

back of block

clip here

Pat's Pointers

Pulling threads to the back. Another way to pull the top threads to the back is to take care of this while the piece is still at the sewing machine. After you have stitched far enough away from the beginning, stop with the needle down. Peek under the fabric to the back of the block. Grab the bobbin thread and gently pull down. This should bring a loop of the top thread to the back. Insert the point of a stiletto into the loop and pull the top thread to the back. Arrange these two threads so they are out of the way and continue stitching the rest of the appliqué piece. I even try to do this with really small circles.

Sewing Order

Stitch all the multiple-layered units first then fuse all the appliqués to the background. Begin sewing with one color of thread and finish all the appliqués in that color. Next, choose another color of thread and finish all the appliqués in that color, and so on until the block is complete. If your block includes straight-stitched bias-strip stems (described on page 28), stitch them last.

Sue's Solutions

Self-threading needle. I use a self-threading needle to bring the top threads to the back of the appliqué block. I think it is easier and quicker than trying to tug them from the back. Sometimes the first stitch has been sewn over slightly, making it even harder to just tug from the back. When stitching is complete, I simply pop the top threads into the needle and thread them to the back of the block. I keep a self-threading needle next to my machine for easy access at all times.

When working on large appliqué blocks, such as those in Sue's MORNING HAS BROKEN (page 73), carefully fold the excess fabric out of the way to make it easier to turn the block at the sewing machine (fig. 20). Folding the block will also keep the fused appliqué piece intact and help keep the background fabric from softening. If the block is scrunched up, the fused appliqué pieces may pull away slightly from the background. If this happens, gently re-iron them in place.

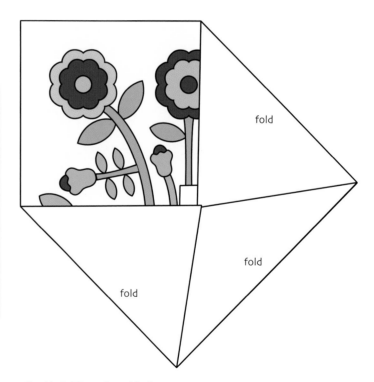

fold

fold

fold

Fig. 20. Folding a large block

The fusible web's job is to seal the raw edge of the appliqué and hold the appliqué to the background for stitching. Ultimately, the stitching is what secures the appliqué to the background. If the block softens during stitching, lightly re-starch from the back.

Sue's Solutions

Durability of fusible web. For a small heart quilt (photo 16), I used all the different brands of fusible web available on the market. The quilt was done in the raw-edge fusible technique. I carefully followed the manufacturer's guidelines for heat settings and lengths of time to heat each product. To test the durability of the appliqué method, the quilt was laundered at least eight times in warm water and placed in a warm dryer. This treatment is more aggressive than quilts should be laundered. The heart quilt has held up extremely well. There is no fraying on the raw edges and no discoloration or other adverse reaction. Preferably, you will want to launder your quilts with care, using a gentle cycle and cool water and letting them air dry. Frequent washings with warm or hot water and drying in a warm or hot dryer may cause wear with any appliqué method.

Photo 16. HEART QUILT (10" x 12"), by Sue Nickels. Different brands of fusible web were used for the raw-edged hearts. This little quilt was washed many times to show that the technique is durable.

Flat Zigzag Stitch

If your machine does not have a blanket stitch, the flat zigzag is a wonderful option for raw-edge fusible appliqué. The satin stitch is another popular choice. However, the stitch length is quite small in the satin stitch. The result is a thick bead of thread along the edge of the appliqué. It is a nice look for clothing but rather stiff for a quilt. The flat zigzag is a better choice because it has a look and feel closer to the blanket stitch. Some quilters like the flat zigzag as well as or even better than the blanket stitch. It can be used in combination with the blanket stitch for some variety in the block.

Setting the Machine

A 50-weight cotton thread in a color matching the appliqué piece looks very nice. The stitch settings will vary from machine to machine. A good place to start is at about a 2.0 width and 1.0 length. The stitch should cover the same area as a blanket stitch, which measures about ¹⁄₁₆" in width. The width should be sufficient to hold the appliqué piece down securely. A stitch width that is too narrow will allow the raw edge to fray, and a stitch width too wide tends to look decorative. The length should be short enough to cover the raw edge but not so short that it has a satin-stitch look.

Practice the stitch on a scrap of fabric. Use an open-toed foot to have a clear view of the stitching. Thread the sewing machine with the same color of thread on the top and in the bobbin. The stitch should follow the edge of the appliqué evenly. The left swing of the stitch should go into the appliqué and the right swing in the background (fig. 21).

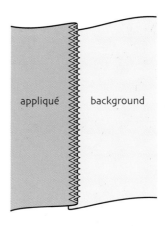

Fig. 21. Flat zigzag stitch

Navigating Curves

When stitching inside and outside curves, it is important to pivot frequently to keep the stitch along the edge of the appliqué.

Pivot in the background fabric (fig. 22). As with the blanket stitch, if your machine has a variable needle position feature, you may want to move the needle to the farthest right setting. Use the right toe of the open-toed appliqué foot as a guide along the edge of the appliqué. Also use the needle down option, if available.

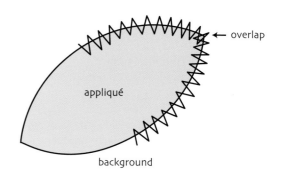

Fig. 23. Stitching an outside point

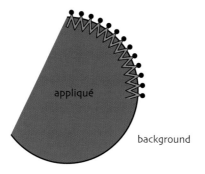

Fig. 22. Pivoting on a curve

Check your stitch for proper tension and adjust it, if needed, as described for a blanket stitch on page 19.

Stitching Outside Points

Sew to the point, ending in the background, pivot and continue stitching. The stitches at the point will overlap (fig. 23).

Stitching Inside Points

Sew to the point, ending in the background. Pivot and stitch into the point. Complete the swing back to the background. Pivot again and continue stitching. It is important to make a stitch into the inside point (fig. 24). Follow the same starting and stopping instructions as described for the blanket stitch on page 21.

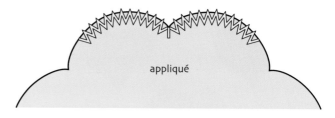

Fig. 24. Stitching an inside point

Included here are the more detailed aspects of fusible machine appliqué. They are really sharp points, really small circles, reverse appliqué, and surface embellishments. Two different options for stems (bias stems and thread stems) will be described, and a unique way to create your own appliqué backgrounds is introduced.

Really Sharp Points

For an appliqué piece that has a really sharp point, the blanket stitch will be too wide and will cross over the point. These overlapped stitches will look sloppy and will make the point appear fuzzy (fig. 25).

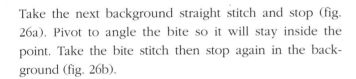

Fig. 25. Overlapped stitches

Here's what to do instead. As you slowly approach the point, you can see where the bite is getting close to crossing over the point. Stop at that spot.

Take the next background straight stitch and stop (fig. 26a). Pivot to angle the bite so it will stay inside the point. Take the bite stitch then stop again in the background (fig. 26b).

Pivot so that the final background stitch goes to the end of the point or even beyond it a bit.

Stop and pivot so the bite will go directly into the point. Take the bite stitch and stop in the background (fig. 26c). Then continue down the other side of the point, stopping and pivoting as before until the bite stitch can once again fit inside the point and be perpendicular to the background straight stitch (fig. 26d).

This method creates a nice sharp point. Even if the thread continues past the point, it helps make the point very precise and, well, pointy! All the stitching helps secure that fragile fabric point as well. See photos 17a and 17b (page 26) for an example of a sharp point handled in this manner.

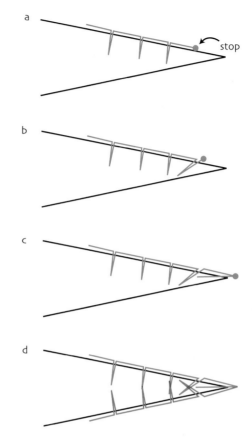

Fig. 26. Progression in fitting stitches to a point

Photo 17a. Crane and Wisteria (20" x 24") by Pat Holly

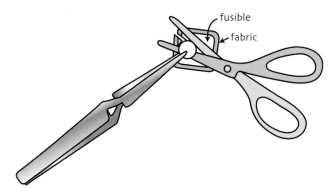

Fig. 27. Using tweezers to hold tiny pieces

Photo 17b. This detail of CRANE AND WISTERIA shows a sharp point with angled stitches on the bird's head feather.

Really Small Circles

Pat says, "I have always loved working with very small things. When I learned to knit as a young girl, I wanted to make smaller and smaller items. There were patterns for tiny sweaters and dresses for Barbie® dolls, and I loved using size zero needles with fingering yarn to make these miniature clothes. For drawing, the smaller the ink pen I found, the more I liked using it. Eventually, even my job as an electron microscope technician involved manipulating objects with an eyelash attached to a glass rod while looking through a microscope. When I discovered how much I enjoyed quiltmaking, I started making smaller and smaller quilts. Here are some of the techniques I use to machine appliqué really small pieces."

Preparing Appliqués

You use the same methods as described in Appliqué Techniques on page 16. At a certain point though, a piece can be too small for cutting out the fusible in the center. You need to have about ⅛" of fusible along the edge of the piece, so if the object is ¼" or smaller, don't cut away any of the fusible from the inside.

After ironing the fusible shape on the back of the fabric, there are some tools you can use to help when cutting out tiny pieces, such as leaves, flowers, and circles. Using very sharp, good quality embroidery scissors, start cutting the fabric piece. When the piece is so small that it is difficult to hold in your fingers (about half way around), use reverse-grip tweezers to hold the object. Place the tips of the tweezers at the area that has already been cut and finish cutting out the tiny piece (fig. 27).

You can use regular fine-pointed tweezers to carefully separate the paper backing from the appliqué piece. It is much easier to slide tweezers between the paper backing and the fabric than to try picking apart the layers with your fingernails. Once you have the pieces prepared, use the fine-pointed tweezers to pick up and place the small pieces on the background. Fuse in place, following the manufacturer's instructions.

Stitching Appliqués

Before you start stitching these small pieces, you need to consider what thread to use. You want the size of the appliqué pieces, the size of the thread, the stitch width, and the stitch length to be in proportion to each other (fig. 28). You would not want to use thread thicker than 50 weight (normal thread). Embroidery cotton is usually 60 weight, and it works well. An excellent choice for tiny pieces is machine embroidery thread. Usually made of polyester or rayon, it comes in wonderful colors and adds a bit of shine to the edge of the appliqué piece.

Fig. 28. The smaller the piece, the finer the thread and the tinier the stitch

Always match the machine needle size to the weight of the thread you are using. For the finer threads, use a 70/10 or even a 60/8 Microtex sharp needle. Because needles should be changed often, it is helpful to keep track of the size of the needle in the machine.

Once you determine the size of thread and needle you will be using, the next step is to set the stitch width and length. When appliquéing small pieces, you need to scale down the size of the stitch. Always sew a few cycles of the blanket stitch to look at its size before working on your actual block.

For a sample, you can use a scrap of fabric 3" x 3". Fold it over to make a rectangle 1½" x 3" (fig. 29). It helps to starch the fabric so you have a smooth, supporting surface.

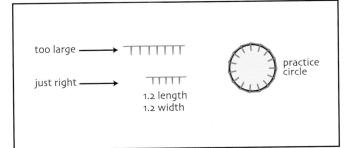

Fig. 29. Test sample

Dial the stitch length and width smaller than normal and sew seven or eight stitch cycles. Adjust the length and width after looking at these stitches.

Try to get the width of the bite about equal to the length of the straight stitch. Use a smaller blanket stitch than usual, such as ⅟₃₂" or even smaller. Some of the circles in our quilts measure about ³⁄₁₆" in diameter. The stitching needs to be small enough to allow some fabric to show in the middle of the piece. Once you have determined the best length and width, write these numbers down on the test fabric for future reference.

When you begin stitching, remember to start with the straight stitch in the background. Get as close to the edge of the piece as possible. When stitching such small objects, you will be stopping to pivot after just about every stitch (fig. 30). Pivot only in the background, usually after the straight stitch and before the bite stitch into the appliqué.

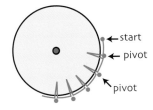

Fig. 30. Pivot points. Notice that the bites aim for an imaginary center (red dot).

This process is pretty much a stitch-by-stitch procedure and must be done slowly. Here's where your needle-down option comes in handy, as well as anything that helps raise the presser foot for the pivot. Fortunately, with such small pieces, it really doesn't take that long to stitch around each one (photo 18). Remember to end with that last straight stitch in the background to allow the top thread to be brought to the back.

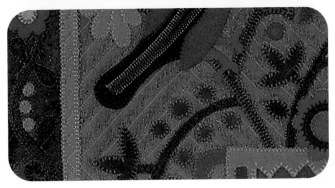

Photo 18. (top) POT OF FLOWERS WITH BIRDS (10½" x 12½"), by Pat Holly. (bottom) Detail shows some really small circles.

With really small pieces, it is more difficult to stop partway around to pull the beginning top thread to the back, but it is doable. If you can't do this (for example, if the top thread has been stitched over and it won't come through when you pull on the bobbin thread), use a self-threading needle to pull the top thread to the back.

Bias-Strip Stems

We often use straight-stitched stems when machine appliquéing. We like to have variety in the stitching throughout our quilt blocks. We also like the dimension these stems give to the surface, almost looking like a real stem. In many of the antique quilts, while most of the appliqué was done by hand, simple stems and vines were often machine appliquéd. A strip of fabric was cut on the bias and the edges were turned. A small straight stitch was then used to attach it to the background.

We use this same idea when doing our bias stems (photo 19). The method works best with stems that are uniform in width. Pat even likes to make tiny bias stems for miniatures. A stem that varies in width is best done with the raw-edge fusible method.

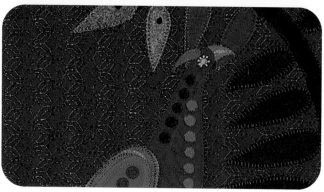

Photo 19 (top) PURPLE BIRD WITH LEAVES (12½" x 12½") by Pat Holly. (bottom) Detail of a bias stem. Note the interesting pattern created by cutting the strip on a diagonal relative to the fabric pattern.

Preparing Bias Strips

Cut bias strips of fabric (fig. 31). A strip width about 1" wide will work nicely. Only small increments in this strip width are needed to adjust the width of the finished stem. Each pattern will indicate the exact width to cut the bias strips, as well as the total length needed.

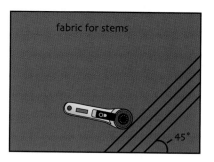

Fig. 31. Rotary cutting bias strips

Refer to figure 32. Fold the bias strip in thirds, overlapping the edges in the center, like a tri-fold brochure. Press the folds and hand baste through all three layers of fabric. Press again firmly to flatten the basted strip.

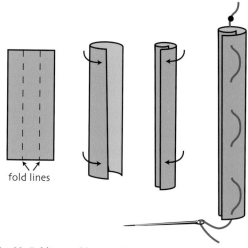

Fig. 32. Folding and basting bias strips

Placing Stems on Background

You will want to baste the stems to the background before fusing any other appliqués. To place the stems, lay the background square over the master pattern, centering it carefully. With a pencil, draw placement lines for the stems on the background. One line drawn down the middle of each stem works well.

If the background is dark or busy, a tracing paper overlay can be used. For this method, carefully cut through the tracing paper down the center of each stem. Lay the tracing paper over the background square, carefully centering it. Use a pencil to draw through the slits to make the placement lines for the stems.

Cut bias strips the proper size. Add about ¼" to the ends of the strips that will lie under other appliqué pieces. Pin the stems in place and thread baste them to the background. Remove pins. Press firmly to flatten the stems. Fuse the remaining appliqué pieces in place.

Stitching Bias Stems

The block is now ready for sewing. The stitching of bias-strip stems should be done after the pieces that lie under them have been stitched. Leave the basting threads in place until the sewing is complete. Use 100 percent cotton thread in a color that matches the stem. Use the same color of thread in the bobbin. Shorten the stitch length slightly and straight stitch along both folded edges of the stem. The straight stitch should be close to the edge (fig. 33). If it is too far away, the fold will have a "lip." If the stitching is too close, it may pull in the folded edge slightly. About ⅟₁₆" from the edge is perfect.

Fig. 33. Stitching bias stems

Many sewing machines have a variable needle position feature. If your sewing machine has it, move the needle to the right until the inside edge of the right toe of the open-toed appliqué foot can be used as a guide. Sew the straight stitch on a practice piece until the stitch length and needle position are where you want them before proceeding.

Starting and Stopping Stitches

After the stem is stitched, bring the top thread to the back of the block. Tie a double knot with top thread and the bobbin thread. If the thread contrasts with the background, the tails should be buried between the background and the stem. An easy way to bring the top thread to the back of the block and to bury the tails is by using a self-threading needle. If the thread does not contrast with the background, clip the tail short after tying the knot.

Other Types of Stems

Sometimes we like to use the same raw-edge technique on stems that we use for other appliqué shapes. If the stem varies in width, is short and wide, or maybe has leaves attached, prepare the pieces as explained for the fusible method (page 17). Fuse in place and use the blanket stitch along the edge of the stem. Continue around any leaves as you come to them (fig. 34).

Fig. 34. Stem with leaves attached

Thread Stems

Another type of stem for attaching leaves or flowers to a vine, or to another stem, is a thin, thread stem. To achieve this look, we use some type of thread for the stem and stitch over the thread with a zigzag stitch. This process is referred to as "couching." Depending on how thin you want your stem, use regular thread or different weights of perle cotton.

Regular thread. Do the following test before stitching on the actual block. Draw a stem line on a well-starched piece of background fabric. For very fine stems, use regular weight thread.

Pull off a length of thread that is eight to ten times the final length of the stem. Double the piece of thread, then double it again so you have four lengths of thread.

Place the sample fabric under the open-toed appliqué foot. Bring the bobbin thread to the top. Lower the needle into the fabric at the beginning of the drawn line. With the needle down, place the thread bundle so that the halfway point is behind the needle and pull the two ends together in front of the needle. It helps to twist these threads together (fig. 35, page 30). You now have a group of eight threads that you will stitch over.

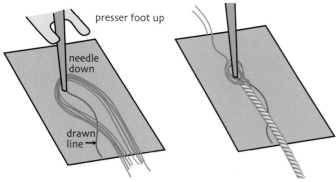

Fig. 35. Threads held around needle, then twisted

Begin to stitch with a zigzag stitch. Adjust the stitches so that the width is just a bit wider than the thread bundle. For the stitch length, the stitches should be close enough together to hold the threads in place. Lay the threads along the drawn line and stitch.

If your stem curves, stop with the needle down on the *inside* of the curve, which will allow you to pull the threads against the needle so they follow the curve (fig. 36).

When you reach the end of the stem, stop and pull out several inches of thread from the needle and the bobbin. Cut these threads, leaving tails about 6" long.

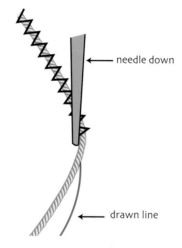

Fig. 36. Couching a curve

Using a self-threading needle, pull the threads to the back and tie off. If the threads are darker than the background fabric and might shadow through, you can weave the thread ends through the bobbin threads before clipping.

Perle cotton thread. For thicker thread stems, try using perle cotton. It comes in different weights, so choose a size that fits your project. You will be stitching over a single strand of the perle cotton.

Cut a piece of perle cotton thread about 6" longer than the stem length.

Lay the perle cotton along the drawn line, leaving 3" extra at the beginning and the end.

Before you begin stitching, pull out 3" to 4" of machine threads (top and bobbin) and hold these threads along with the perle cotton end when you start to sew.

Use regular-weight thread in the machine that matches the perle cotton and adjust the stitch length and width to cover it. Then zigzag over the perle cotton (fig. 37).

Fig. 37. Couched perle cotton

Finish the thread tails by pulling the top threads to the back. With a very large-eyed needle, like a sharp tapestry needle, pull the perle cotton tail to the back of the work also.

If the thread is difficult to put through the eye of the needle, here is a technique that may help: Cut an 8" piece of regular thread. Fold it in half and pass the folded end through the needle's eye. A loop will be formed on one side of the needle's eye. Place the thick thread through the loop and use the thread loop to pull the thick thread through the eye (fig. 38).

Fig. 38. Threading perle cotton through a needle

If you think the threads will show through to the front, thread all the ends into a large-eyed needle. Bury the threads between the background and a nearby appliqué piece or carefully slide the needle under the bobbin zigzag stitches and pull the threads through then trim (fig. 39). If they won't show, knot the regular threads with the perle cotton thread and trim them all to about ½".

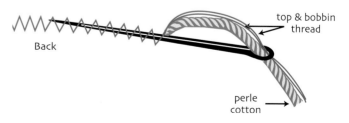

Fig. 39. Sliding thread ends under bobbin zigzag stitches

If you have intersecting stems and vines, stitch the stems that will be under the vines first (fig. 40).

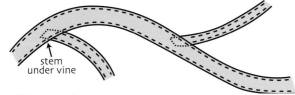

Fig. 40. Stems under vine

For thread stems, you can either make them first and then add the appliqué or wait to sew the stems until after the appliqué has been stitched (fig. 41).

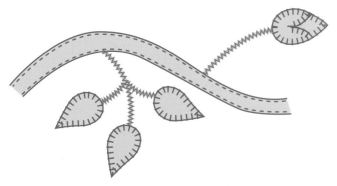

Fig. 41. Thread stems, bias-strip vine, and appliquéd bud

Reverse Appliqué

There are many places where reverse appliqué can be very attractive. The Leaf and Bud block contains good examples of reverse appliqué (photo 20). For this method, the stitching is still done along the raw edge, but the raw edge is not where we expect to see it. It is inside the flower.

Photo 20. The Leaf and Bud block from Morning Has Broken has several reverse-appliqué shapes. The full quilt and the pattern are on page 73.

One reason we might choose reverse appliqué is that we like the look of it. Another reason might be to reduce bulk and the number of layers of fabric in the quilt. The Rose block has a good example of a multiple-layered rose for which reverse appliqué was used effectively (photo 21 and fig. 42).

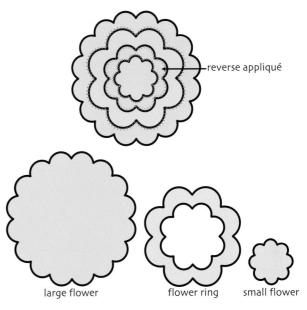

Fig. 42. Multiple-layered unit with reverse-appliqué flower ring

Photo 21. In the three large flowers in this Rose block from Morning Has Broken, the second ring of petals from the center is reverse appliquéd.

Preparing Reverse Appliqués

The following instructions are for a flower that has two reverse-appliqué shapes in the center (fig. 43, page 32).

These inner shapes are cut out of the flower and underlays of fabric are inserted.

Fig. 43. Reverse-appliqué flower

On the paper side of the fusible, trace the flower shape from the master pattern and add the ¼" outside the line and the scant ¼" inside the line as usual (fig. 44).

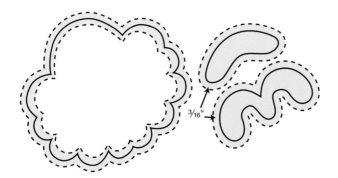

Fig. 44. Fusible open shape for whole flower

Trace the inner shapes and add ¼" to the outside of both shapes. Draw thin strips (bridges) between the outer and inner shapes, so that all the fusible pieces are attached to each other (fig. 45). Cut the fusible shapes out with their bridges.

Fig. 45. Fusible open shape with bridges shown in red

Lightly starch the back of the fabric for the flower. Fuse the open shape to the back of the fabric, following the instructions for the specific fusible web used. With small embroidery scissors, cut on all drawn pattern lines. Your fabric appliqué piece will have two holes in it.

Remove the paper from the underlay areas, but leave the paper on the outside edge of the flower. Cut the fabric for the underlays to fit the holes plus at least a ¼" allowance all around (fig. 46). Fuse the underlay fabrics to the flower.

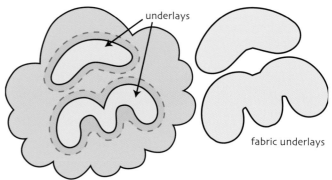

Fig. 46. Cut fabric underlays larger than the cutout areas.

Blanket stitch around the underlay fabrics (fig. 47). The reverse appliquéd flower is now ready to appliqué to the background.

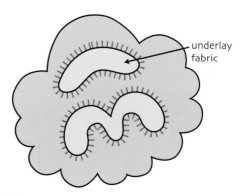

Fig. 47. Blanket stitch the reverse-appliqué raw edges.

Sue's Solutions

Underlay tip. You can pull away the papers from the two underlays and use them as patterns for cutting the fabric pieces.

SURFACE EMBELLISHMENTS

Adding thread embellishments to your quilt can really enhance its design. Here's a chance to use those pretty built-in embroidery designs on your sewing machine, or you can use free-motion stitching to add excitement to individual appliqué pieces or finished appliquéd blocks. You can even create embellished fabric to use for your block backgrounds.

Embellishing Background Fabric

Look through your machine embroidery stitches to find some candidates for creating your own embroidered background fabric.

Preparing Fabric

Most of the time, no matter what you are embellishing, you need to prepare the fabric before you stitch. If you machine embroider complicated patterns on the fabric with no support, the stitches will probably bunch up and pucker the fabric.

Most machine embroidery is done with a tear-away or water-soluble stabilizer placed on the back of the fabric. For stitching embroidery motifs, this is the best way to get a smooth result. If you want to do an overall pattern on the fabric, however, that type of stabilizer is too difficult to remove. Instead, you can starch the background fabric so it is stiff as a board (well, a piece of paper). This will act as a stabilizer.

Choosing Stitches

Decide what stitch and thread you want to use. Pick the appropriate needle to match the thread. You can use 50-weight cotton thread in the bobbin, and you can match the bobbin thread color to the top thread or to the background fabric. Test to see what look you like for your project.

Cut a fabric piece 2" wider and longer than the finished size needed for your block background. To plan your embroidery, it helps to draw parallel guidelines on the fabric piece with removable pencil or chalk. Draw the lines ½" apart or whatever distance works with your design.

If you want to keep your decorative stitch at the same point in the stitch cycle for each row, draw a line perpendicular to the guidelines at one end of the fabric (fig. 48). Start each row on the starting line and at the same point in the stitch cycle. This is a good time to use the pattern-begin feature if it's available on your machine. It does take a while to stitch a large area, so get comfortable!

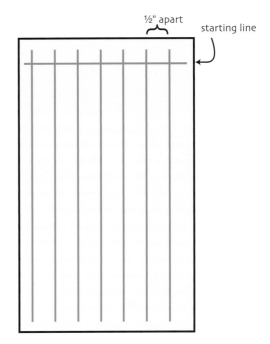

Fig. 48. Drawing guidelines

Try to keep your bobbin full. If you do run out in the middle of a row, undo enough stitches to pull the top thread to the back and make a knot. Undo the stitches to a point in the stitch pattern that you recognize and start up again from that point.

When planning a pattern, remember that just adding lines of straight stitching can be very effective. You can also stitch on top of a previous row to change the look. This is when you may realize that there are endless possibilities and that you can make truly unique textiles.

Stitching Order

The stitching order will depend on the stitches you have chosen. If you are making a piece of fabric and using guidelines as shown in figure 48, stitch the first pattern in every other row to keep the fabric from getting stretched out of shape. Sew the second pattern between the first rows (fig. 49).

Fig. 49. Alternating rows

After stitching the background with your design, the fabric may have lost some of its crispness. It is okay to starch it again. Be careful to use the correct heat setting on the iron if you have used synthetic threads like poly-

ester or rayon. It works best if you just spray the starch and iron it on the back. You can also spray with plain water then iron, which will cause the starch to re-activate, so you can avoid adding more starch.

Place the appliqué pieces on the background and stitch. The only other thing to consider is how you will quilt the background areas that have this added decorative stitching. It's probably best to keep the quilting simple and stitch between the lines of the surface thread work.

Free-Motion Embroidery

Sue first used surface embellishments on her quilt LE PANIER DE FLEURS (photo 22, page 35). She thought this two-color quilt needed some extra threadwork to add interest. With free-motion stitching, she added curlicues, little flowers, tendrils, and much more. It looks very nice, and it is much more visible on the surface as an embellishment than it would have been as free-motion quilting.

The embellishments on our patterns are indicated by red lines, but feel free to come up with your own ideas. Before embellishing, the block needs to be stabilized. If

Pat's Pointers

Stitching a sampler. After purchasing a wonderful new machine several years ago, I decided to spend a few days just exploring and playing with it. There were many styles of fancy stitches, so I stitched samples of many of the designs. I wanted to see what the different stitches actually looked like. Sometimes the little drawing on the machine or in the book looked different in person, or I was surprised by the size and scale of a stitch. I decided to create a reference book for these stitches, and I use it whenever I want to choose stitches for a project.

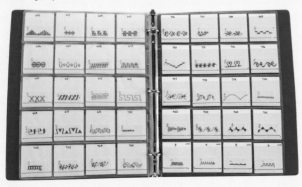

I used dark thread and stitched on pieces of index cards. I cut each card to fit into the little pockets meant to hold photographic slides and wrote on the card any information I would need to find that stitch again. Some machines number the different stitches so you can use that for reference. I used a couple of different machines, so I needed to keep track of what stitch came from which machine. It really didn't take that long, and it was a fun project to see all the things my machine could do.

If you decide to make a sample book like this, don't limit your stitches to those labeled as "decorative." Some of the so-called utility stitches make great designs. Even a simple zigzag can be the perfect addition to your project. Remember, you can also change the way a stitch looks by varying the width and length. Some machines let you mirror-image the pattern or reverse the design from top to bottom. Some wonderful "plaid" patterns can be made with a simple straight stitch by varying the thread type and color.

the starch has worn off while appliquéing, you may need to lightly starch it again. Then position the block over the master pattern and, using a fabric marking pencil, lightly trace the stitching guidelines on the block.

Photo 22. (top) LE PANIER DE FLEURS (67" x 78"), by Sue Nickels. (bottom) Detail: Free-motion threadwork adds surface interest.

Practice free-motion stitching before using it on your block. For a practice piece, prepare a scrap of fabric by starching it lightly. Thread the machine with your choice of thread. A 40- or 50-weight, 100 percent cotton thread in a contrasting color looks nice. Use the same thread in the bobbin. Attach a darning foot and lower the feed dogs.

It is helpful to use something on your fingers to help move the block easily. Fingertips cut from kitchen rubber gloves work great. Start at the edge of the appliqué piece. Lower the presser foot. Next, take one stitch to bring the bobbin thread to the top of the block. Hold both the top and the bobbin threads and begin free-motion stitching, following the marked line. Stop stitching at the end of the design. Try to achieve smooth, even stitching as you would with free-motion quilting.

Using a self-threading needle, bring the threads to the back of the block. Tie a double knot. If these threads will show from the front of the block, weave them into the stitching on the back (fig. 50). Clip the thread ends short.

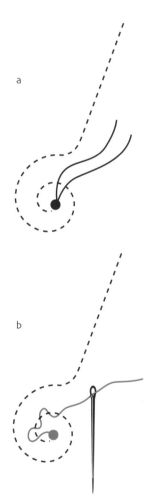

Fig. 50. Two ways of ending stitching on the back of the block: (a) tie knot and clip threads, (b) tie knot, weave thread ends, then clip.

Check the tension carefully. Because the work is done on one layer of fabric, the tension may need adjustment. If the bobbin threads are showing slightly on the top, loosen the top tension.

Decorative Stitch Embellishment

You can also embellish the surface by using the blanket stitch as a decorative feature. Adjust the stitch width longer and use contrasting thread. Instead of placing the stitch on a raw edge, reverse the stitch so the bite is in the opposite direction (fig. 51).

Once you have practiced your embellishments, you can move on to your appliqué block. See figure 52 for an example of using multiple rows of decorative stitches to enhance a piece. This stitching takes time, and it's a bit like hand embroidery work. Much of the time is spent working with the thread ends, but it is worth the time spent and the result is fabulous.

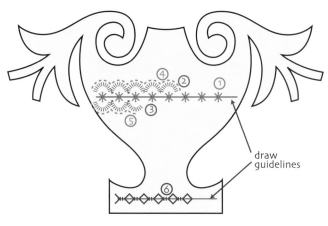

Fig. 52. Surface embellishment on vase

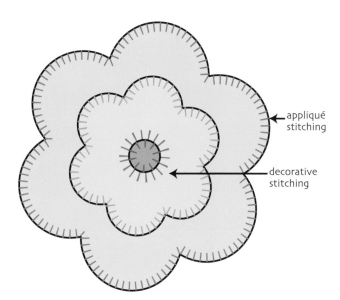

Fig. 51. Using the blanket stitch for decoration

In the Tulip and Berries Basket block from MORNING HAS BROKEN (page 73), blanket stitching was used to create the berries (photo 23).

Photo 23. Tulip and Berries Basket block from MORNING HAS BROKEN

We would like to share with you some of the different edge treatments we have discovered and used on our quilts. There will be directions along with each of the projects that include measurements specific to each quilt. Some of these finishing concepts we consider to be advanced techniques because of the sewing skills required. Please read through all the directions before beginning. We recommend that you try a sample of a technique before attempting to add it to your quilt.

Following the directions for the finishing technique you have chosen, use a rotary cutter to square the corners and trim the edges of your quilt in preparation for finishing the edges.

Sue's Solutions

Trimming a quilt. A small quilt can be placed directly on a large rotary mat. Use a rotary ruler and cutter to trim the outside edge. A large quilt can be placed on the floor to see if its edges are even. Then place the rotary mat on the floor under the quilt, moving the mat as needed, to trim the outside edge.

Basic Binding

Some of the quilt projects in this book have a single-fold binding as part of a special edge treatment. You can use either straight-grain or bias-grain binding for the single-fold technique (fig. 53). We use bias binding for a check or plaid fabric because we like the look of these fabrics on the bias. Choose a straight-grain binding if you are running low on the fabric you want to use for the binding.

Measure around the outside edge of the quilt to determine the total length of binding needed. Cut strips 1¼" to 1½" wide for a single-fold binding. Sew them together, end to end, on the diagonal to make one long continuous strip the length needed. Press the seam allowances between the strips open. The binding is ready to be sewn to the quilt.

Arrange and fold (package) the quilt with the bulk of the fabric to the left of the machine. Use thread that matches the color of the binding, a straight stitch, and if desired, a walking-foot attachment.

Leave about 5" of the binding loose and start sewing along one side of the quilt, about one quarter of the way from a corner. Sew with an accurate ¼" seam allowance, following the edge of the quilt as a guide. The binding should fit snugly. As you sew, smooth the binding, a little taut, along the edge of the quilt. Hold the binding firmly while sewing to keep it flat and smooth.

To miter the binding corners, place a pin at the ¼" point from the end of the quilt (fig. 54). Sew to this point and backstitch a few stitches. Cut the threads and fold the binding back at a 90-degree angle as shown. Fold the binding again to align it with the next side of the quilt.

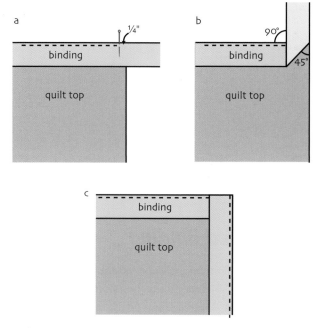

Fig. 54. Mitering the corners: (a) sew to the pin, (b) fold the binding at an angle, (c) align the binding with the next side.

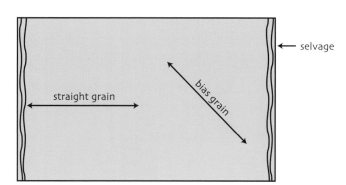

Fig. 53. Straight and bias grains

Repackage the bulk of the quilt and sew the next side. Continue to sew, mitering the remaining corners as before. End the stitching, leaving about 4" of binding end unsewn.

Measure carefully and join the binding ends on the diagonal. Press the seam allowances open. Finish sewing the rest of the binding to the quilt (fig. 55).

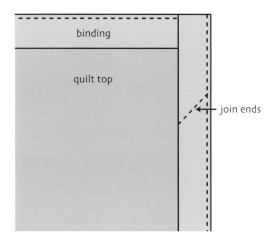

Fig. 55. Join binding ends on the diagonal and finish sewing them to quilt.

Bring the binding to the back of the quilt and hand stitch, carefully turning the edge under ¼". Miter the corners on the back of the quilt and hand stitch (fig. 56).

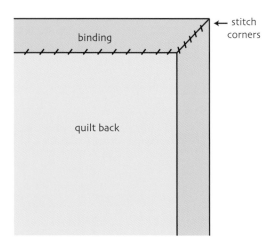

Fig. 56. Sew the miters closed.

Embellished Binding

This is a regular binding except the fabric is embellished with decorative stitches before being cut into strips and sewn to the quilt. Embellishing fabric takes a bit of time, so you may want to reserve this technique for your smaller projects.

To make embellished fabric for binding, refer to Surface Embellishments (page 33), which explains how to prepare the fabric and do the actual stitching. The only difference, when using embellished fabric for binding, is figuring out how large an area to prepare. To do this, measure the outside edge of your quilt after it has been quilted. Add about 12" to allow for mitering the binding at the corners and overlapping the ends.

To calculate the size of the rectangle of fabric needed, divide the length of the binding by 18" (a convenient size) and multiply the resulting number by 2. For example, if you need 92" of binding (enough for a 20" square quilt), 92" divided by 18" is 5 (rounded off); 5 times 2 is 10". So cut a rectangle 18" by 10".

Because embellishment adds extra bulk to the fabric, it is best to use a single layer for binding, with strips cut 1¼" to 1½" wide. Piece the strips together, end to end, to add up to the length you calculated.

If you want the embellishing stitches to end up on an angle to the edge of the quilt, draw guidelines on the rectangle at a 45 degree angle to the selvage (fig. 57). Following the guidelines, embroider the rectangle, alternating the direction you stitch to compensate for sewing on the bias. Cut the binding strips parallel to the selvage.

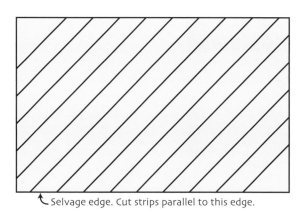

Fig. 57. Fabric rectangle with 45-degree guidelines

Sew the bias strips together, end to end, to form one long strip. Follow the directions for basic binding to finish the edges of the quilt.

Piping

Using piping will add a bit of color and dimension along the edge of your quilt (photo 24, page 39). Piping is a fold of fabric sewn into a seam. Cording encased in fabric and used in the same way is also called "piping." We have used many different sizes of cording to make piping, from teeny tiny for a miniature quilt to quite large cording for a big quilt. Here we will explain how to add piped binding to a normal-sized wallhanging or quilt.

Photo 24. (top) ALBERD VICTORIUS (24" x 20"), by Pat Holly. (bottom) Detail: Notice the purple piping next to the binding.

For making your own piping, you can purchase cording in the upholstery trim department of a fabric store. It comes in different sizes, so pick whatever size you think fits your project. For most quilts, we use cord that is ³⁄₃₂" wide.

You can use cord made of any material. Cording for curtain or window shades is made of polyester or rayon, and it is particularly stable. Use this type of cord if your project needs stability. For miniature quilts, we have used cord as small as gimp thread, which is used for tailoring.

Preparing Piping

Cut strips of fabric to cover the cording. If your quilt has a curved edge, you will need the flexibility of bias grain to follow along the edge. If the piping goes along a straight edge, you won't need to use bias. For a straight edge, cut the strips across the width of the fabric, perpendicular to the selvage. When you cut in this direction, the fabric still has a slight amount of give to it. If you want the fabric to be perfectly stable with no give at all, cut the strips parallel to the selvage.

Pat's Pointers

Fabric give. The amount of give in a fabric is a result of how it was woven. The threads parallel to the selvage are the warp threads, and they are stretched tight on the loom. The threads that cross the warp are called weft threads. Because a weft thread goes over and under the warp threads, there's a bit more thread in that direction. As a result, the cross grain has a slight give when pulled.

Make four separate pieces of piping, one for each side of the quilt. Measure the sides, top, and bottom of the quilt and add about 2" to each measurement to find the lengths of the fabric strips needed to cover the cording. Cut strips of fabric 1¼" wide and piece them together, end to end, as needed to make the four strips. Trim the seam allowances to about ⅛" and press open.

Fold each strip in half, right side out, along its length. Lay a piece of cording in each strip along the fold, pushing the cord as close to the fold as possible. Using a zipper foot and a basting-length stitch, sew each strip as close as possible to the cording (fig. 58). Trim the seam allowances to about ¼".

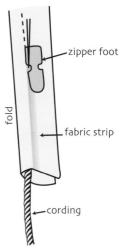

Fig. 58. Machine sewing piping

Adding Piping to a Quilt

After the quilt has been quilted, trim the edge, leaving a ¼" seam allowance all around. Trim the batting and backing ¼" beyond the seam allowance (fig. 59).

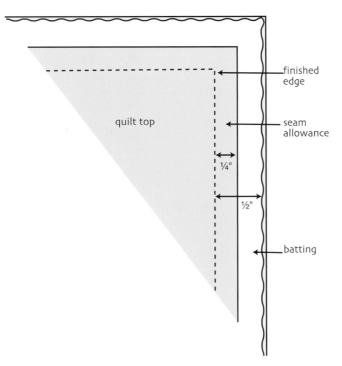

Fig. 59. Trimming the batting and backing

Add piping to the sides of the quilt first. Align the raw edge of the piping with the raw edge of the quilt top and pin (fig. 60). Use a zipper foot to baste the piping in place, stitching as close to the piping as possible.

Fig. 60. Piping pinned to quilt

After the side piping strips have been attached, add the top and bottom piping, overlapping them at the corners. If you don't like the thickness of the overlap, stop stitching about 2" from the end. Carefully open up the fabric covering the cord and undo the basting stitches to reveal the end of the cord. Trim off the end as needed to fit. Resew the fabric around the cord and lay the fabric down so the now cordless end overlaps the side piping, and stitch.

Trim ¼" from the batting and backing all around so it is even with the quilt top. Add binding in the usual manner, referring to Basic Binding instructions on page 37. Use the zipper foot and stitch the binding as close as possible to the cording (fig. 61). If you have trouble getting close to the the cord, try pressing your fingernail along the piping, through the binding fabric. This causes the binding fabric to crease right next to the bump of the piping and gives you a guideline to stitch along.

Fig. 61. Stitching binding over piping

After sewing, check the right side of the quilt to make sure the piping basting stitches are not exposed. Mark exposed areas with pins and stitch again, trying to stitch between the piping and the previous stitching line. Finish the binding on the back, following the Basic Binding instructions.

Decorative Cording

You can use purchased decorative cording with an attached seam allowance, sometimes called "lip cord." Lip cord was used for FOLKY FEATHERS AND FLOWERPOTS (photo 25). You can find this product in the upholstery department of a fabric store.

Wait to trim the backing and batting until after the cording has been sewn to the quilt.

Photo 25. Detail: FOLKY FEATHERS AND FLOWERPOTS by Pat Holly (full quilt on page 65). Lip cord was used to finish this quilt.

This technique can be used to insert different edge treatments between the top and backing of your quilt, such as rickrack, lace, ruffles, fringe, or anything else you can think of. Purchase enough decorative cording, of the type that has a seam allowance, to go all around the edge of the quilt plus some extra (12" is plenty).

The quilt should be quilted before you add the edge treatment. So there is room to maneuver when inserting the cording, be sure to leave an area unquilted that is about 1" from the finished edge of the quilt. You can quilt that area after the cording has been added, if you like.

To add lip cord to your quilt, first fold the batting and backing out of the way. Pin them, if necessary, to hold them out of the way of the top layer. Trim the cording allowance so it is just ¼" from the cord itself (fig. 62).

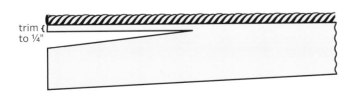

trim to ¼"

Fig. 62. Trimming the cording seam allowance

Attaching Cording

To attach the cording, start in the middle of one side of the quilt. Align the edge of the cording seam allowance with the raw edge of the quilt top. Use a zipper foot and move the needle to the far-left position. Begin stitching a little ahead of the cord then move onto the cording itself (fig. 63).

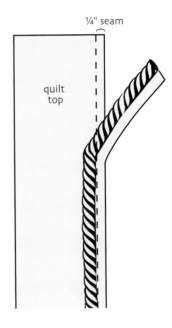

¼" seam

quilt top

Fig. 63. Beginning to stitch the cording

Stitch along the ¼" seam line, keeping the cord seam allowance and the edge of the quilt top even. If you find that you are not getting close enough to the cord, try using an open-toed appliqué foot. It will fit over the cording, and by adjusting the needle position, you can get closer to the cord (fig. 64).

Fig. 64. Using an open-toed appliqué foot to attach cording

When you are ¼" from the corner, stop and pivot the cording to continue along next edge. Make a clip in the cording seam allowance to release it and allow it to make that turn (fig. 65).

Fig. 65. Clipping the corner

Continue stitching around the entire quilt. When you come back to the beginning, overlap the cording at an angle (fig. 66). Trim the ends so they are even with the edge of the quilt.

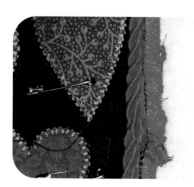

Fig. 66. Overlapping cording ends

Pat's Pointers

Continuous piping. If you are using continuous piping all around the quilt edges instead of decorative cording, attach it in the same manner as for the lip cord but start and stop like this: Begin stitching about 1" from the end of the piping, leaving that 1" free. Stop stitching about 2" from the other end. Open up the fabric by removing the basting stitches. Do this on both ends to expose the cord. Line up the cord ends and cut them so the two ends butt together. Trim the fabric on one side so there is a ½" overlap. Turn the edge under ¼", close the fabric, and stitch along the ¼" seam line.

Finishing the Back

Release the batting and backing if you had them pinned out of the way. Trim the batting and backing ¼" from the edge of the cording seam allowance on all sides of the quilt (fig. 67).

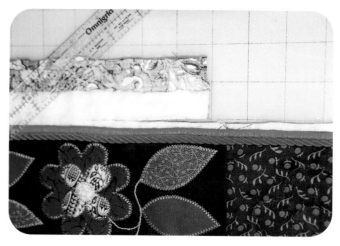

Fig. 67. Trimming the edges

Turn ¼" of the backing over the batting, with the folded edge as close to the cording as possible. The cording seam allowance should be hidden in between the layers, and the corners will be slightly rounded. Pin in place (fig. 68). Continue to pin the backing in place all around the edge of the quilt.

Fig. 68. Pinning the backing

Stitch from the front of the quilt and use a zipper foot to get as close as possible to the edge of the cording (fig. 69, page 43). You could also stitch the backing down by hand, if you prefer.

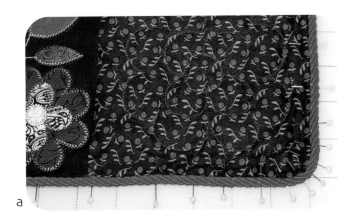

Fig. 69. Preparing to stitch: (a) pinned edge (front view), (b) stitching with a zipper foot from the front.

Loopy Edge

This edge treatment is a fun and different way to finish your quilt. Once you get the basic idea, you can make the loops any size you want and even change their shape by how you attach the loops to the binding. Please read through all of these directions. If you make a practice piece first, it will help you understand the concept. We will explain the basic idea, using two different fabrics and alternating them for the loops (photo 26). You can use all the same fabric for both loops, if you like.

Photo 26. Detail: TWENTY-ONE BIRDS by Pat Holly. Photo of full quilt on page 62.

You will need to plan the number of loops for your project. Draw the outline of the quilt on a piece of graph paper, using the graph squares to represent real measurements. Pick a loop size that is in proportion to your quilt. If the loops are too small, they will be tricky to make and a headache to attach. In the example, the loops are 4" apart and 2" high. Add the loops to your graph paper drawing then count how many loops you need (fig. 70).

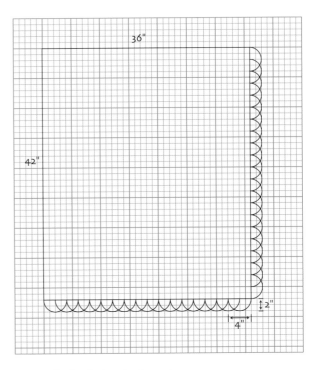

Fig. 70. Graph of quilt showing loop placement

Preparing Loops

Make your loops from fabric cut on the bias. The stretch in the bias cut will allow the loops to curve easily. For TWENTY-ONE BIRDS (page 62), the fabric strips were cut 1½" wide. Make a sample loop to determine how long each loop needs to be, as follows: Cut a strip longer than you think you need. Fold the strip right sides together along its length. Sew the strip with a ¼" seam allowance to make a tube. Trim the allowance to ⅛".

Carefully turn the tube right side out with a turning tool then finger-press it flat. Work on a surface that has a marked grid, such as a rotary-cutting mat with grid lines. Refer to figure 71 (page 44). Starting at one end, tape the end of the loop in place. Curve it around in a half-circle with the top of the circle at the 2" mark. Bring the other end to just inside the 4" mark. Trim the loop ends to extend ¼" beyond the base line. Take the loop off the grid and measure it. This is how long each loop needs to be. For TWENTY-ONE BIRDS, this was 6¼". Multiply this measurement by how many loops you need, to calculate the total length to make.

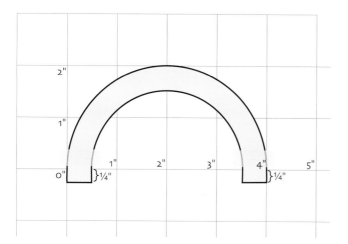

Fig. 71. Determining loop length

Adding Loops to Binding Strip

The loops will be sewn to strips of fabric that will act as the binding for the quilt. Make eight lengths, two for each side of the quilt. Cut the strips 1½" wide and about 4" longer than each side's measurement.

The easiest way to attach the loops to a binding strip is to lay the strip, right side up, on the grid. If you don't have a grid, make pencil marks every 2" along the edge of the strip. Start about 2" in from the end of the strip. Place one end of a loop even with the long edge of the strip, as shown in figure 72. Have the loop seam face the inside of the curve. Curve the loop so that the other end is 4" away. Pin the loop in place.

Fig. 72. Placing the first set of loops

Continue to place the rest of the loops along this strip. Be sure the loops are butted right up next to each other. It's okay if the loops do not lie completely flat. The bias grain will allow them to be pressed into the curved shape. When all the loops have been pinned in place, take the strip to the ironing board and pin it down (fig. 73). Carefully position the loops so they make nice curves. Give the whole strip and loops a gentle pressing.

Fig. 73. Loops pinned to ironing board

Take the strip, with loops still pinned in place, back to the grid and place them so they line up with a grid line again. For the second layer of loops, start the first loop 2" over and pin the end in place. The other end will be placed 4" away, but don't just lay it on top of the first layer of loops. Slip the end under the previous layer so the loops are intertwined. Continue down the length of the strip (fig. 74). Press this layer the same way as the first.

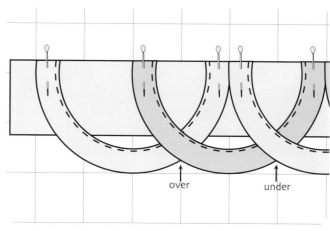

Fig. 74. Second layer of loops

Sewing Binding to Quilt

Lay the second strip of binding fabric on top of the strip with the pinned loops, right sides together. Sew the strips together with a ¼" seam allowance as shown, enclosing the loops (fig. 75). Open the strips and press them with the seam allowances away from the loops. Carefully press the loops flat and in the correct half-circle shape.

When you quilt the layers, be sure to leave about 1" from the edge of the quilt unquilted. Trim the edges of the quilt, leaving a ½" seam allowance. Starting with the two sides of the quilt, check to see if the loop binding strips fit the quilt. If the loops at the ends of a strip are not lining up within ½" of the quilt edge, undo the stitching and make any

small adjustments needed by shortening or lengthening these end loops. Stitch the strips together again. Trim the loop binding, at both ends, to ½" beyond the loops.

Open up the binding strips. With the loops facing the quilt top, line up the edge of the binding strip with the trimmed edge of the quilt. Pin the strip to the quilt. Stitch the binding to the quilt with a ½" seam allowance (fig. 76). Press so the strip is flat against the quilt.

Bring the other side of the binding to the back of the quilt. Turn under ½" of the edge of the binding. Fold the edge down again so that the fold covers the raw edge. Be sure the folded edge covers and extends beyond the stitching (fig. 77, page 46).

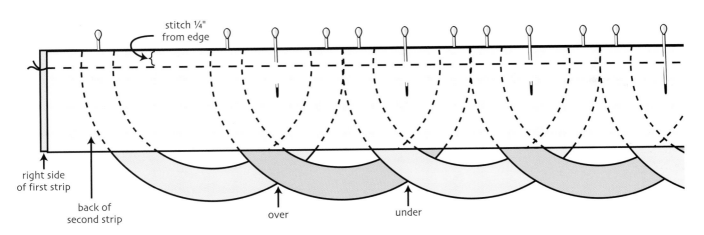

stitch ¼" from edge

right side of first strip

back of second strip

over

under

Fig. 75. Sewing strips together

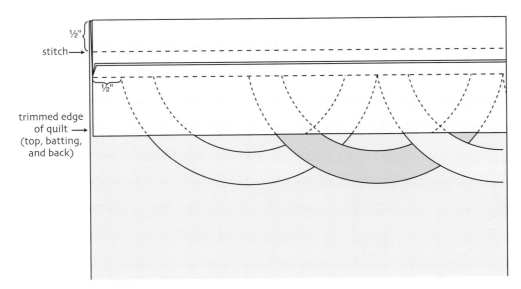

½"

stitch

½"

trimmed edge of quilt (top, batting, and back)

Fig. 76. Stitching the binding to the quilt top

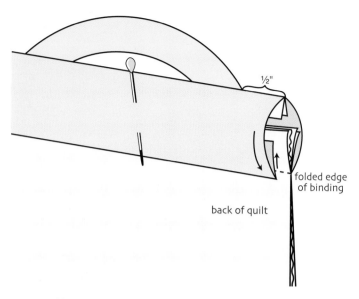

Fig. 77. Fold the binding to cover the raw edges.

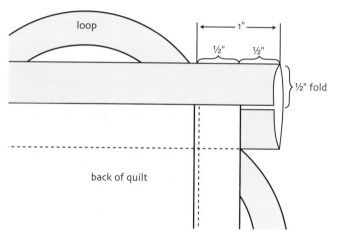

Fig. 78. Trim the binding ends, leaving ½" to fold under.

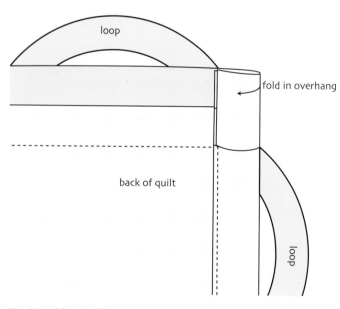

Fig. 79. Fold in the ½" extensions.

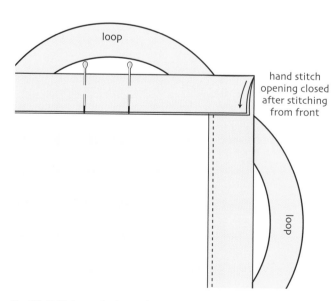

Fig. 80. Fold down the long edge.

Stitch in the ditch from the front of the quilt, securing the back of the binding. If you want, you can hand baste the folded edge then stitch from the front. Or, you can hand appliqué the back of the loop binding as you would for a traditional binding. Repeat for the other side of the quilt.

Before you attach the bottom binding, check to be sure it fits. The loops should end ½" inside the edge of the quilt. Trim both ends of the binding strips 1" beyond the edges of the loops. Open up the binding strip and pin it to the quilt edge. The ends of the strip should extend ½" beyond the outer edge of the side binding. Stitch the bottom binding in place with a ½" seam allowance. Press the strip flat against the quilt. Fold the long edge over ½" and press (fig. 78).

Fold in the ends of the binding over ½" (fig. 79). Then fold the long edge over again (fig. 80). Stitch as you did for the side bindings. Slip-stitch the small openings closed.

To add the top binding, which does not have any loops, sew two strips, right sides together, along one long edge. Turn the strip right side out and press. Attach the sewn strip to the quilt in the same manner as the bottom binding. The top binding will look the same as the other three sides, just without the loops.

Scalloped Edge

This unique edge treatment adds a wonderful finish to a classic-style quilt like MORNING HAS BROKEN (page 73). Sue first used this edge on a floral appliqué quilt called LE PANIER DE FLEURS (page 35). On that quilt, she used a double scallop, which would be easy to incorporate in your own quilt projects once you are familiar with the basic concept.

MORNING HAS BROKEN (page 73), which has a single-scallop edge treatment, is used as the example for the steps in the method. Please read through all the instructions before starting on your edge.

Planning Scallops

When quilting the layers, sew a line of straight stitching ½" from the edge of the quilt around all sides.

1. Decide which corner scallop treatment you would like to use. The corner can be done with a circle element, or the scallops can end flush at the corners (fig. 81).

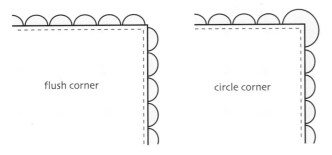

flush corner   circle corner

Fig. 81. Corner treatments

2. Find the finished length and width of your quilt. (It is important to use measurements taken after the layers have been quilted to allow for shrinkage.)

MORNING HAS BROKEN *is square, and the length and width are 60".*

3. On a strip of paper of suitable length, use your measurement to draw a straight line representing the edge of your quilt.

4. Decide on the spacing you would like to use for your scallops.

My scallop spacing is 2".

5. Place marks along the line to represent the scallop spacing. If you have decided to use a circle element for the corner, figure this into the measurements to determine how many scallops you will need.

I marked every 2" on the paper strip, which makes 30 scallops.

6. Using a circle maker, find the half-circle size that fits in the scallop space, leaving a ⅛" space between scallops for ease of turning (fig. 82).

I used a 1⅛" circle for my scallops.

Cutting and Sewing Scallops

1. Use the circle maker to mark two scallops on your paper strip. Then use these two scallops to make a template in heat-resistant plastic. Include a ½" allowance along the bottom of the template. This template will be used later for pressing the sewn scallops. It can also be used to mark the half-circles on the fabric.

2. To determine the width of the fabric strips you need to cut, measure the height of your scallop (half its diameter) and add at least 2" to this measurement. The extra width

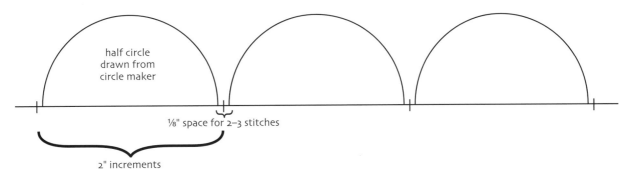

half circle drawn from circle maker

⅛" space for 2–3 stitches

2" increments

Fig. 82. Scallop spacing

will make it easier to handle the strips as you sew the scallops.

3. For the strip length, add 4" to the measurement of the quilt edge.

4. Use the measurements from steps 2 and 3 to cut two strips of fabric for each side of your quilt.

I cut my fabric strips 3" x 64".

5. On the wrong side of one fabric strip, draw a straight line ½" from a long edge. This is the base line for the scallops. Mark the scallop spaces 2" apart on the line, starting in the center and working toward both ends.

6. Using the circle marker or heat-resistant template, mark half circles on the line, leaving ⅛" between scallops (fig. 83). These marks are the stitching lines.

7. Place the marked fabric strip on top of the other fabric strip, right sides together. Pin securely.

8. Use a shortened straight stitch (about 1.5 setting on most machines) to sew all the scallops. When stitching the curves, pivot often to keep the stitching line smooth.

9. Use two to three stitches in the ⅛" space between scallops. These stitches are important because they help create a little space for turning the strip smoothly.

10. Use pinking shears to trim closely along the scallops. Clip into the area between scallops as shown in figure 84.

11. Turn the scallops right side out. Place the heat-resistant template inside the scallops and press them very flat.

12. Carefully trim the seam allowances to ¼" from the bottom of the scallops (fig. 85). Repeat for the remaining three sides of the quilt.

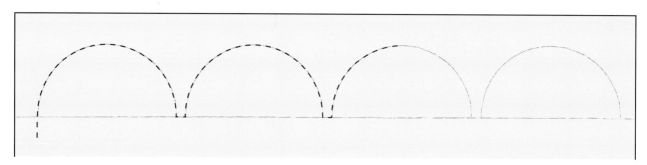

Fig. 83. Mark the half circles on the line and stitch.

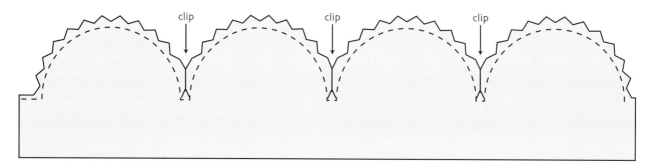

Fig. 84. Pink the edges and clip the seam allowances.

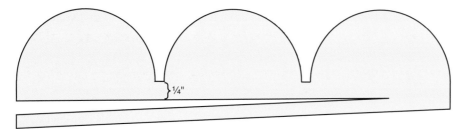

Fig. 85. Trim the bottom edge, leaving a ¼" allowance.

Sew Scallops to Quilt

1. When quilting the layers, machine sew around the quilt ½" in from the edge as described previously.

2. Carefully trim away the batting at this sewn line.

3. Insert the ¼" allowance of the scallops between the ½" seam allowances of the quilt. Turn ¼" of the quilt allowance under. Use a small appliqué hand stitch to sew the turned edge to the scallops (fig. 86).

4. In the same manner, hand stitch the back. Repeat for all four sides.

Corner Element

1. If your plan requires a corner scallop, use the same method to cut and sew an individual scallop for each corner.

2. Insert the corner scallops into the ½" seam allowances and sew as before (fig. 87).

Double-Scalloped Edge

1. Prepare the front row of scallops as described previously.

2. Prepare a second row of scallops in the same manner, but these will be offset from the front row. The drawn straight line needs to be 1" from the edge of the fabric strip.

3. After pressing the turned scallops, carefully trim the seam allowance to ½" from the bottom.

4. Baste both scallop strips together, aligning the cut edges. The back scallops will be ¼" higher than the front ones (fig. 88). Attach these scallops to the quilt in the same manner as a single-scalloped edge.

Fig. 86. Sewing the turned edge

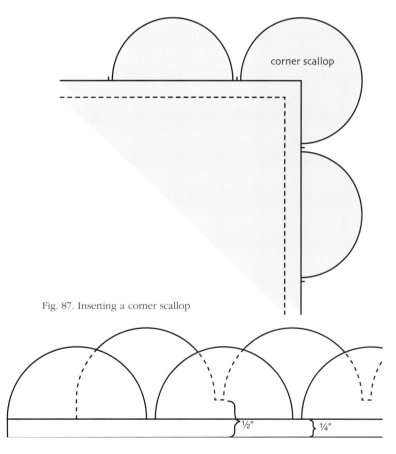

Fig. 87. Inserting a corner scallop

corner scallop

Fig. 88. Aligning the rows

½"   ¼"

Quilt 13" x 13"
Finished block 9" x 9"

TRUE BLUE BIRDS by Pat Holly.
Notice that machine embellished fabric
was used for the binding.

New Skills to Try

Materials

Piece	Size
Block background	11" x 11"
Scalloped border	13" x 13"
Outer border	15" x 15"
Flowers and birds	scraps
Vase	5" x 7"
Backing	15" x 15"
Batting	15" x 15"
Binding	12" x 27"

Block Appliqué

The pattern on page 54 is given full size. It is a reverse image for tracing the appliqué patterns on paper-backed fusible web.

1. As they are needed, cut the pieces listed in the Materials table.

2. Using the raw-edge fusible method, make a master pattern and prepare the appliqué pieces.

3. If desired, add thread embellishment to the vase piece. Be sure the fabric is well-starched first.

Pat's Pointers

Adding embellishment. Add thread embellishment after the piece is cut out so you know where to start and stop the stitching. You can start and stop inside the edge of the piece or start at one edge and continue stitching off the edge on the other side. If the knotted thread ends are on the edge of the piece, be sure to tuck them under when you fuse the piece to the background.

4. Stitch the multi-layered units. For example, the flower centers can be fused and blanket stitched to the flower petals, the birds' eyes can be reverse appliquéd, and the bird parts can be fused together (fig. 1).

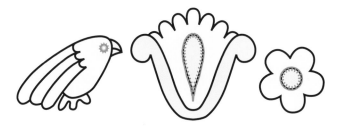

Fig. 1. Appliqué units

5. Place the prepared units and the rest of the appliqué pieces on the background and fuse. Stitch all of the edges. Use thread stems to connect the three small circles to the birds' heads.

Borders

There are three parts to connect to complete the quilt top: the appliquéd block, the fused inner scalloped border, and the outer border.

1. Prepare the inner scalloped border by tracing the whole border (page 54) on fusible web.

2. Cut ¼" away from the scallop line. Without cutting through the drawn line, carefully cut into the inner area and cut it away, ¼" from the drawn straight line (fig. 2).

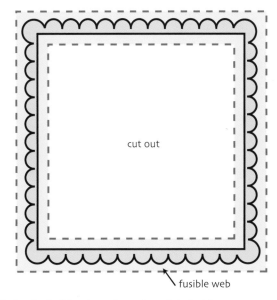

cut out

fusible web

Fig. 2. Cut the fusible where shown by red dashed lines.

3. Fuse the shape to the wrong side of the 13" scalloped-border square (fig. 3). Cut the scalloped edge on the drawn line. Cut out the inner square on the drawn line.

Fig. 3. Fuse the shape to the scalloped-border square.

4. Before fusing the scalloped border to the block, carefully cut away part of the paper backing all around the inner edge to expose about ¼" of the edge, which is the part to be fused to the block background (fig. 4). If the paper backing starts to separate from where you need it to stay, carefully press the paper back in place. Don't let the iron touch the area where the paper was removed.

Fig. 4. Trimming paper backing from the inside edge

5. Position the scalloped border on the block, both right side up, and fuse in place. Stitch along the inner straight edge of the scallop border with the blanket stitch (fig. 5).

Fig. 5. Stitching the inner edge of the scalloped border

6. Turn the piece over and trim away the excess background fabric, exposing the other side of the scalloped border (fig. 6).

Fig. 6. Trim the excess background. (Note: some of the paper backing has already been removed.)

7. Press and starch the outer border square. Completely remove the paper backing from the scalloped border.

8. Position the block on the outer border fabric. Fuse in place and use a blanket stitch to attach the scalloped edge (fig. 7, page 53).

Fig. 7. Fuse block to outer border fabric and stitch.

9. Carefully cut away the extra border fabric behind the block (fig. 8).

Fig. 8. Cut away the center area of the border fabric.

10. Trim the finished piece to 13½" square.

Finishing

1. Layer the quilt top with batting and backing. Baste the quilt layers.

2. Bind the quilt's edges with basic binding (page 37) or use embellished binding.

Embellished Binding

For this quilt, the binding piece was stitched on a skewed rectangle whose guidelines were drawn parallel to the selvage. I made enough for about 60" of 1¼" wide binding. The binding was attached as described in the basic binding section (page 37).

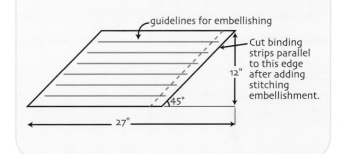

True Blue Birds **full-sized pattern (right-side flower)**

For raw-edge appliqué, cut fused fabric pieces on the line.

TRUE BLUE BIRDS *full-sized pattern*
For raw-edge appliqué, cut fused fabric pieces on the line.

RA

center

left flower

Flower pattern on page 53

THE FAB FOUR by Pat Holly. This quilt has surface
embellishment on the background and a piped binding.

THE FAB FOUR

New Skills to Try

Materials

Piece	Size
Block background	17" x 19"
Bias stems	10" x 18", cut 1" wide strips
Birds, flowers, and leaves	scraps
Pieced border	
	8" x 14" each of 2 colors (a light and a dark)
Piping	1¼" x 2¼ yds
Cording for piping	2¼ yds
Backing	18" x 22"
Batting	18" x 22"
Binding	1¼" x 2¼ yds

Background Embellishment

1. Complete the surface work on the background rectangle. If you choose to have a plain background, proceed to Block Appliqué.

2. To create the diamond pattern, draw guidelines across the middle of the fabric in both directions.

3. From the center out, make marks every ⅝" along the width. Mark every 1¼" along the length (fig. 1).

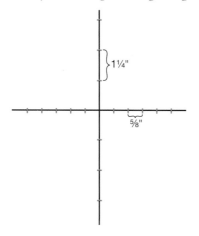

Fig. 1. Mark ⅝" on horizontal line and 1¼" on vertical line.

4. Connect the marks to make the diamond guidelines (fig. 2).

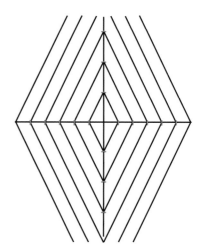

Fig. 2. Connect the marks.

5. Stitch all over the surface of the background (fig. 3). Feel free to make up any sort of pattern you like.

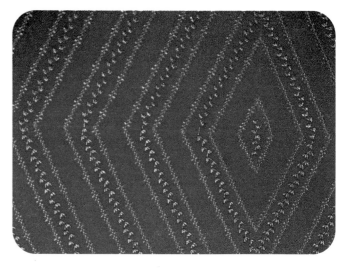

Fig. 3. Finished background (close-up)

Block Appliqué

The patterns on pages 59–61 are given full size.

1. As they are needed, cut the pieces listed in the Materials table.

2. Following the raw-edge fusible method, make a master pattern and prepare the appliqué pieces.

3. Create multiple-layered units of the birds and flowers. Stitch the reverse-appliqués in the units, such as the eyes (fig. 4, page 57).

Fig. 4. Appliqué units

4. Use 1" bias strips to prepare a bias stem 80" long. Using the photo of the quilt as a guide, pin the bias stem in place.

5. Fuse and stitch the appliqué pieces that go under the stem (fig. 5). Straight-stitch both sides of the stem.

Fig. 5. Units that go under the stem

6. Place and fuse the rest of the appliqué pieces. Blanket-stitch the edges, being careful to match the size of the stitch to the size of the appliqué. Use the thread-stem technique to stitch the bird legs.

7. Trim the block to 13½" x 17½", which includes seam allowances.

Pat's Pointers

Appliqué sequence. I like to stitch all of one color at a time (do all the reds, for example, then all the blues, and so on). If some of the appliqué pieces start to come loose, carefully re-fuse them. If you use threads other than cotton, be sure your iron is not too hot because it may damage or even melt the threads.

Checkerboard Border

1. Cut strips 1½" x 8", nine from each of the two colors (18 strips total).

2. Sew the strips together as shown, alternating the two colors (fig. 6). Press seam allowances open.

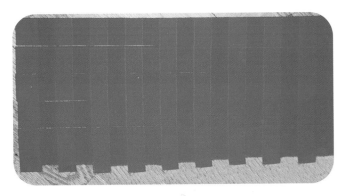

Fig. 6. Join strips, alternating the colors.

3. Cut four border strips 1½" wide across the pieced fabric (fig. 7).

Fig. 7. Cutting border strips

4. Because you need only 17 squares for each side border strip, remove the last light square by undoing the stitching. The side strips will then start and end with dark squares. Sew these strips to the quilt and press the seam allowances toward the center (fig. 8).

5. For the top and bottom strips, you need only 15 squares. Remove three squares from each strip so they start and end with light squares. That way, the colors will continue to alternate around the corners (fig. 9). Sew the strips to the quilt and press the seam allowances toward the center.

Finishing

1. Layer the quilt top with batting and backing.

2. Quilt the layers. To quilt a background that has been embellished with thread, you can use the stitching as guidelines and quilt in between those rows. Fancier quilting will not show up well.

3. Use your favorite method to bind the raw edges of the quilt or follow the directions on page 38 for adding a piped binding.

Fig. 8. Adding side borders

Fig. 9. Adding top and bottom borders

full-sized patterns
For raw-edge appliqué, cut fused
fabric pieces on the line.

full-sized patterns

For raw-edge appliqué, cut fused
fabric pieces on the line.

RA

RA

← suggestion
for legs

Quilt 40" x 46" (including loops)
Finished block 6" x 6"

TWENTY-ONE BIRDS by Pat Holly. Loops were added
to three sides of this quilt.

TWENTY-ONE BIRDS

New Skills to Try

Materials

Piece	Size
Block backgrounds (2 colors, ½ yd. ea.)	10 squares 7" ea. color
Border (1 yd.)	sides: 6½" x 30½"
	top & bottom: 6½" x 36½"
Vine (1 yd.)	2½" (bias) x 5½ yds.
Flowers and birds	scraps or fat quarters
Backing	1½ yds.
Batting	40" x 46"
Binding	½ yd.
Loops (2 colors)	½ yd. ea. color

Appliquéing the Blocks

The patterns on page 64 are given full size.

1. As they are needed, cut the pieces listed in the Materials table.

2. Using the raw-edge fusible method, make a master pattern and prepare the appliqué pieces.

3. Fuse and stitch the multiple-layered units (birds, wings, feet, and beaks). Make the eye of each bird with a contrasting color, using reverse appliqué.

4. Fuse the appliqués to the background squares and stitch. Trim the blocks to 6½" square.

5. Use the thread-stem technique to attach the little dots to the birds' heads.

Quilt Assembly

1. Sew the blocks together, alternating the background colors. Make five rows of four blocks.

2. Add the side borders, then the top and bottom borders.

Border Appliqué

1. Follow the directions for making straight-stitch bias stems to make the vine for the border.

2. Position the vine on the border, following the quilt photo for guidance. Keep the vine at least ½" from the quilt edge. Pin it in place then baste down the center of the vine. Overlap the ends and stitch them together.

3. For the appliqué, prepare 20 leaves, cutting half of them in reverse; 55 dots; and the twenty-first little bird.

4. Place the leaves, dots, and little bird around the border. Remember to keep the appliqué pieces at least ½" from the quilt edge. Position the leaves so the stem ends go under the vine. Fuse in place and stitch the vine edges.

Finishing

1. Layer the quilt top with batting and backing and quilt the layers. If you will be adding loops, leave 1" all around the edge unquilted.

2. Bind the quilt's edges with basic binding (page 37) or use looped binding.

full-sized patterns

FOLKY FEATHERS AND FLOWERPOTS by Pat Holly. Pat added thread stems and a corded edge to this charming wallhanging.

FOLKY FEATHERS AND FLOWERPOTS

New Skills to Try

Technique	Page
Raw-edge fusible machine appliqué	16
Thread stems	29
Layered appliqué units	31
Corded edge (optional)	41

Materials

Piece	Size
Block & border background (1¼ yds.)	
	4 blocks 12" x 12"
	4 borders 6½" x 20½"
Corner squares (¼ yds.)	4 squares 6½" x 6½"
Leaves, flowers, vases, and birds	scraps
Perle cotton for stems	1 package
Upholstery lip cord	4 yds.
Backing (1⅛ yds.)	36" x 36"
Batting	36" x 36"

Block and Border Appliqué

The patterns on pages 66–72 are given full size.

1. As they are needed, cut the pieces listed in the Materials table.

2. Using the raw-edge fusible method, make a master pattern and prepare the appliqué pieces.

3. Assemble and stitch any appliqué units that can be layered (flowers with centers, for example). The birds' eyes are cut out and reverse appliquéd. Use the thread stem method for thin stems.

4. Place the prepared units and the rest of the appliqué pieces on the background and fuse. Stitch all of the edges. Trim the blocks to 10½" x 10½".

5. Cut six large and three small flowers for each border strip. Cut an assortment of leaves in various sizes. Each border can be slightly different.

6. Using the photo of the quilt for a general idea of placement, arrange the pieces on the border strips. Be sure to keep the appliqué pieces at least ½" from the edge.

7. Fuse the flowers and leaves in place on the border and stitch. Use the thread-stem method and perle cotton to make stems.

Quilt Assembly and Finishing

1. Sew the blocks together in two rows of two.

2. Add the side borders then sew the corner squares to the ends of the two remaining borders. Sew these to the top and bottom of the quilt.

3. Layer the top, batting, and backing and quilt the layers. For the corded binding, be sure to keep the quilting stitches at least 1" from the outer edge of the quilt. This area can be quilted after the corded edge is completed.

4. Add cording edging, if desired, or finish as described for basic binding on page 37.

FOLKY FEATHERS AND FLOWERPOTS full-sized patterns for borders

RA →

center →

full-sized patterns

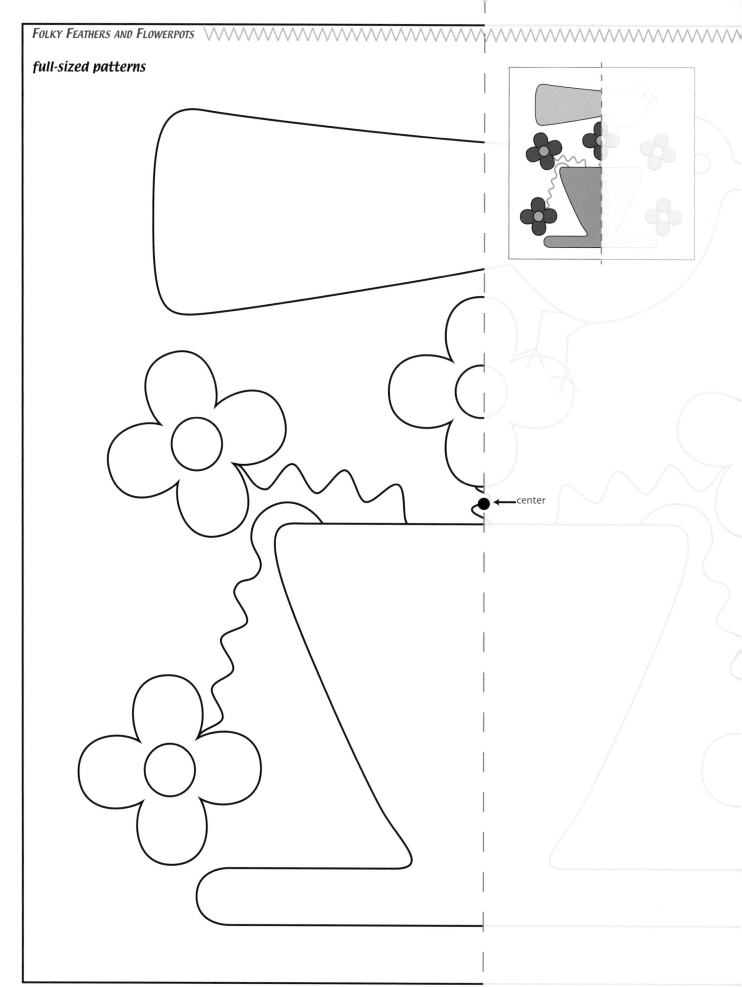

center

full-sized patterns

center

full-sized patterns

center

← center

full-sized patterns

center

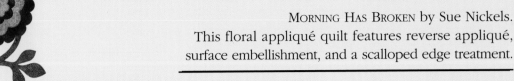

Quilt 62½" x 62½"
Finished block 14" x 14"

MORNING HAS BROKEN by Sue Nickels.
This floral appliqué quilt features reverse appliqué,
surface embellishment, and a scalloped edge treatment.

MORNING HAS BROKEN

The quilt design was inspired by an antique quilt made around 1850. There are five different block patterns. Four of them are used twice. The patterns are given full-size, starting on page 76. Note that four of the patterns are given in reverse image for the fusible method.

New Skills to Try

Materials

Piece	Size
Block backgrounds (2½ yds.)	9 squares 17" x 17"
Sashing and Border (1¾ yds.)	12 strips 1½" x 14½"
	4 squares 1½" x 1½" (cornerstones)
	4 strips 1½" x 48" (border 1)
Border 2 (2 yds.)	4 strips 7¾" x 65"
Appliqués (4 yds.)	total patterns on pages 77–93
Backing (4 yds.)	2 panels 34" x 64"
Batting	64" x 64"
Scalloped edge (1½ yds.)	8 strips 3" x 64"
Thread	avg.-wt. cotton for appliqué and piecing; matching cotton thread for quilting; optional surface work: fine cotton matching background

Sue's Solutions

Surface work. The result is meant to be subtle. I used rows of straight stitches and curvy stitches on each block then added flower and leaf embroidery between the rows.

Come up with your own unique ideas; be creative! Remember to test the embroidery first on a small practice piece. Please note: the four corner blocks have diagonal lines. Change the direction of the stitching every other row to eliminate shifting caused by sewing along the bias.

Background Embellishment

1. Complete the surface work on the background squares. If you choose to have a plain background, proceed to Block Appliqué.

2. For the surface stitching, use a chalk pencil to mark guidelines 1" apart on the block background squares (fig. 1). Fill the whole 17" square with these guidelines.

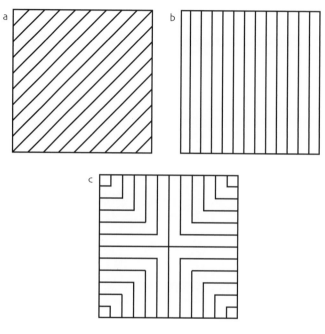

Fig. 1. Block guidelines: (a) four corner blocks, (b) four side blocks, (c) center block.

3. Using a fine cotton thread in a color matching the background, stitch the surface work on each block.

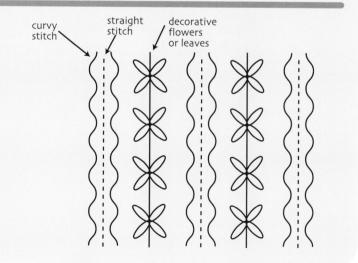

curvy stitch   straight stitch   decorative flowers or leaves

Sue's Solutions

Orientation. Remember to position the appliqué in the correct orientation relative to the surface work on the background. This is most important for the corner blocks.

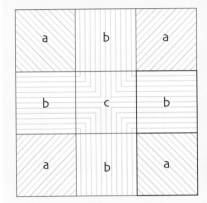

Placement of appliqués relative to surface work

Block Appliqué

To avoid confusion, we recommend that you work on one block at a time.

1. As they are needed, cut the pieces listed in the Materials table.

2. Following the raw-edge fusible method, make a master pattern for each block and prepare the appliqué pieces.

3. Create any multiple-layered units and stitch the reverse-appliqués in the units.

4. Use 1" bias strips to prepare bias stems. An approximate length of 8 yards of bias, from a variety of fabrics, is used for the stems.

5. Using the tracing paper pattern as an overlay, position the stems. Baste the stems to the background

6. Carefully position all appliqué pieces and fuse in place.

7. Blanket-stitch all fused appliqué pieces. Stitch by thread color (all red, then all green, etc.). Straight-stitch the edges of the bias stems last.

8. Add surface embellishments, if desired, following the red placement lines.

9. Repeat the instructions to make the following blocks:
  one Stars and Flower (center)
  two Rose and Buds Basket
  two Tulip and Berries Basket
  two Leaf and Buds (corner)
  two Triple Rose (corner)

10. Trim the blocks to 14½" x 14½", which includes seam allowances.

Quilt Assembly

1. Assemble the blocks, sashing, and cornerstones as shown in the quilt assembly diagram (fig. 2).

2. For each side of the quilt, sew the inner border and outer border together. Add the combined borders to the quilt and miter the corners.

Finishing

1. Layer the quilt top with batting and backing and quilt the layers. For a scalloped edge finish, stitch a straight line ½" from the edge. Stop all quilting at this line. The quilted area is 7" wide (fig. 3). For basic binding, leave the traditional ¼" seam allowance.

2. Measuring 7½" from the outer border seam, trim the quilt on all four sides. Be sure the corners are square.

Scalloped Edge

1. Referring to the scalloped-edge instructions on page 47, prepare four scalloped-edge strips with thirty half-circle scallops (fig. 4). Use the 1⅞" half-circle pattern on this page.

2. Carefully follow the scalloped-edge instructions to finish the edge.

Fig. 2. Quilt assembly

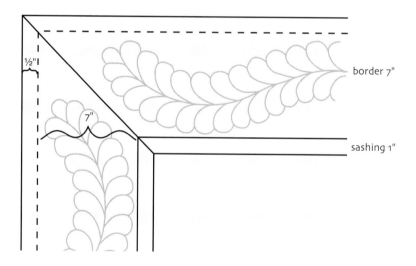

border 7"

½"

7"

sashing 1"

Fig. 3. Machine stitch ½" from the quilt edge.

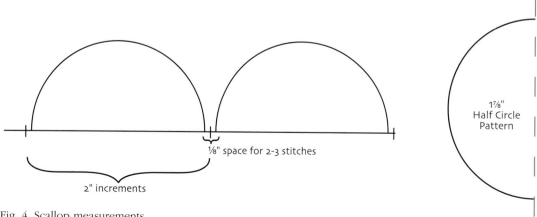

⅛" space for 2-3 stitches

2" increments

1⅞"
Half Circle
Pattern

Fig. 4. Scallop measurements

STARS AND FLOWERS CENTER **full-sized pattern**

RA

center

ROSE AND BUDS BASKET *full-sized pattern*

center

Rose and Buds Basket **full-sized pattern**

center

ROSE AND BUDS BASKET **full-sized pattern**

center

STITCHED RAW EDGE APPLIQUÉ • SUE NICKELS & PAT HOLLY

Rose and Buds Basket **full-sized pattern**

center →

TULIP AND BERRIES BASKET *full-sized pattern*

center

STITCHED RAW EDGE APPLIQUÉ • SUE NICKELS & PAT HOLLY

Tulip and Berries Basket *full-sized pattern*

center

TULIP AND BERRIES BASKET *full-sized pattern*

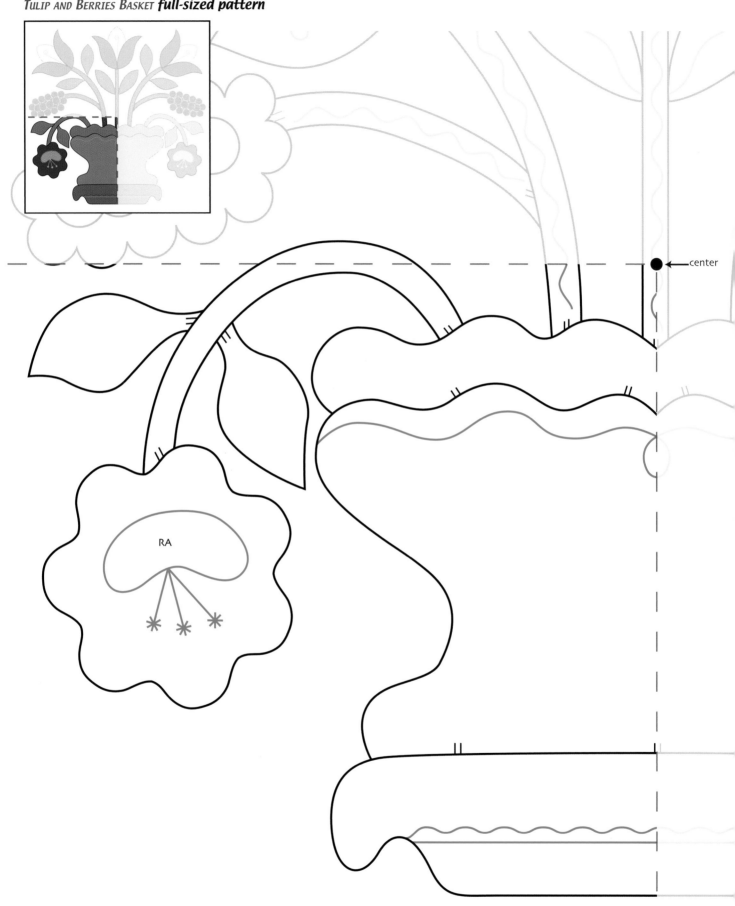

RA

center

STITCHED RAW EDGE APPLIQUÉ • SUE NICKELS & PAT HOLLY

TULIP AND BERRIES BASKET **full-sized pattern**

center →

RA

LEAF AND BUDS CORNER *full-sized pattern*

center

LEAF AND BUDS CORNER **full-sized pattern**

center →

LEAF AND BUDS CORNER *full-sized pattern*

center

RA

RA

RA

STITCHED RAW EDGE APPLIQUÉ • SUE NICKELS & PAT HOLLY

Leaf and Buds Corner **full-sized pattern**

center →

RA

TRIPLE ROSE CORNER *full-sized pattern*

RA

center

Triple Rose Corner **full-sized pattern**

RA

center →

TRIPLE ROSE CORNER *full-sized pattern*

center

RA

STITCHED RAW EDGE APPLIQUÉ • SUE NICKELS & PAT HOLLY

TRIPLE ROSE CORNER *full-sized pattern*

center →

Authors' Favorite Tools

We have researched these products and are confident of the success achieved with them. There are other products that work, but these are the ones we like the best with our techniques. Most products are available at quilt shops.

Paper-backed fusible web – Lite Steam-A-Seam® by The Warm Company

Fabric marking pencils – Roxanne™ Quilter's Choice

Scissors – Elan 4" embroidery

Curved-tipped scissors – Tooltron

Spray starch – Niagara®, regular weight

Template plastic – Templar®, heat resistant

Tweezers – Tooltron

Self-threading needles – EZ Quilting® or Clover®

Sewing machine needles – Schmetz

Thread – Mettler® 100% cotton 50 weight and 60 weight

> Superior King Tut Quilting Thread™ 100% cotton 40 weight
>
> Sue Nickels' tone-on-tone colors
>
> Superior Masterpiece 100% cotton 50 weight
>
> Robison-Anton Super Brite® Polyester machine embroidery thread

Bernina® Sewing Machines.
Pat's 170QE and Sue's 200QE were used for the quilts in this book. They have the features mentioned in the supplies section to make machine appliqué easier.

ABOUT THE AUTHORS

Pat has been sewing almost her whole life, beginning with sewing clothes as a young girl. She is a graphic artist and attended the University of Michigan School of Art & Design. She also spends time volunteering for her daughter Alyssa's theater endeavors, including costume work for local productions.

Sue also has been sewing much of her life and was an art major in college at Eastern Michigan University. She has pursued a professional career in quilting for the past 15 years.

The sisters enjoy working together on quilts as well as patterns and books. They live about a three-hour drive from each other and find creative ways to manage working together on projects. Sue travels extensively, teaching machine techniques, and Pat will join Sue occasionally, especially for international trips. This has been a wonderful working relationship. Pat and Sue work so well together because they both love the connection with quilters of the past and enjoy the technology of today.

Pat Holly

Sue Nickels

OTHER AQS Books

This is only a small selection of the books available from the American Quilter's Society. AQS books are known worldwide for timely topics, clear writing, beautiful color photos, and accurate illustrations and patterns. The following books are available from your local bookseller, quilt shop, or public library.

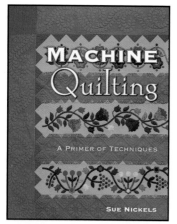

#6299   us$24.95

#6903   us$19.95

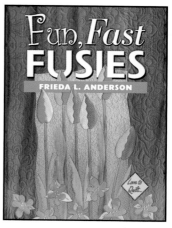

#6801   us$19.95

#5855   us$22.95

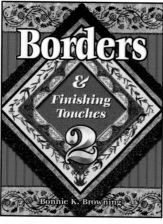

#6804   us$22.95

#6676   us$22.95

#6904   us$21.95

#6674   us$19.95

#6896   us$22.95

LOOK for these books nationally. **CALL 1-800-626-5420** or **VISIT** our Web site at **www.AmericanQuilter.com**